An Altitude
SuperGuide

Walks and Easy Hikes in the Canadian Rockies

An Altitude
SuperGuide

Walks and Easy Hikes in the Canadian Rockies

Graeme Pole

Altitude Publishing
Banff Alberta Canada

Photo, front cover: Peyto Lake from Bow Summit.

Photo, front cover inset: Professor Charles Fay, 1919. Photographer, H. Pollard. Whyte Museum of the Canadian Rockies.

Photo, back cover: Lower Falls, Johnston Canyon

Photo, overleaf: Moraine Lake Rockpile

Copyright © 1992
Altitude Publishing Ltd.
Post Office Box 490
Banff, Alberta
Canada T0L 0C0

Extreme care has been taken to ensure that all information in this book is accurate and up to date, but neither the author nor the publisher can be held legally responsible for any errors that may appear.

Canadian Cataloguing in Publication Data
Pole, Graeme, 1956–
Walks and easy hikes in the Canadian Rockies
Includes bibliographical references and index.
ISBN 0-919381-96-0
1. Trails–Rocky Mountains, Canadian (B.C. and Alta.) – Guidebooks.* 2. Hiking – Rocky Mountains, Canadian (B.C. and Alta.) – Guidebooks.* 3. Rocky Mountains, Canadian (B.C. and Alta.) – Guidebooks.* I. Title.
FC219.P64 1992   917.11'044
C92-091206-0   F1090.P64 1992

Editor: John F. Ricker

Maps: Debbie Jow

Design: Robert MacDonald, MediaClones Inc., Toronto, Banff, and Vancouver, Canada

All photographs not credited here are by the author.

Printed and bound in Canada by Friesen Printers

For Marnie, companion on and off the trail

Acknowledgments

The author gratefully acknowledges research assistance provided by the following people with the Canadian Parks Service: David Palmer at the Western Region Library, Calgary; Kevin Van Tighem and Terry Arnett; Larry Halverson, Kootenay National Park; Heather Dempsey and Dave Gilbride, Banff National Park; Joanne Cairns, Edwin Knox, and Rob Watt, Waterton Lakes National Park; Wes Bradford and interpretation staff, Jasper National Park; Harry Abbott, Yoho National Park; and Paul Cinnamon, Mt. Robson Provincial Park.

Cia and Ben Gadd kindly opened their Jasper home to a couple of tired truck campers during a spell of poor weather, and didn't kick us out when it became sunny again. They also offered a wealth of information concerning Jasper National Park. Thank you, Cia and Ben.

Most of all I would like to thank my wife, Marnie, for her devotion to the fieldwork, the tireless editing of the the manuscript, and the help in co-ordinating the project. The hiking schedule was often dictated by the need to acquire photographs at particular times of day. It was a schedule only a photographer would follow without complaint, and meant rising early, backtracking often, and frequently waiting interminably for the sun to peer through the clouds during a summer of fickle weather. Even on repeat visits to the same location, Marnie remained patient and enthusiastic. Her organizational skills and penchant for making lists kept the author from coming adrift in a raft of scribbled field notes. Thank you Marnie.

With royalties from the sales of this book, the author is financing the planting of three trees for each tree used in the production.

Contents

The Walks and Easy Hikes

Appendices

Preface

Welcome to the Canadian Rockies. These mountains are renowned worldwide as a destination for hikers. This reputation is undeniably based on the remarkable scenery revealed from the highways and the network of more than 3000 kilometres of backcountry trails in the Rocky Mountain parks. Lesser known are the more than 100 comparatively short and easy frontcountry trails, accessible from roadsides and townsites. Though solitude may be difficult to find on trails close to the highway, much of the scenery that awaits the casual walker is as spectacular as that which lures the backpacker far into the hills.

In compiling this volume, the author had the pleasure of hiking every one of these trails, many of them more than once. In total, they represent the spectrum of topography, vegetation, wildlife, and climate that makes up this extraordinary mountain landscape. If you hike every trail, you will see: 30 glaciers, 92 lakes, 39 waterfalls, and 13 canyons, as well as 4 hot springs, and half a dozen alpine meadows. There are wonderful opportunities for viewing wildflowers, birds, and other wildlife.

The blessing is that these trails grant us easy access to a wonderland. The curse is that the trails readily show evidence of our passing, unless we learn to tread lightly. Please read: **A Trail Etiquette** and **What to Wear and Carry.** Do your part to help preserve the mountain parks of the Canadian Rockies.

Your comments about using this guidebook will be appreciated by the author and the publisher. Happy walking and hiking.

Please note: Throughout this book, the term "Rockies" refers to the area between Waterton Lakes National Park and Mt. Robson Provincial Park. The pronunciation of some words is indicated in parentheses. The stressed syllable is capitalized.

What to Wear and Carry

The hiking season in the Rockies is generally from late May to early October at lower elevations, and from late June to mid-September higher up. Be sure to inquire about trail conditions at a park information centre, especially if you will be hiking early or late in the season.

Street shoes can be worn for some of the short walks, but for most outings, you should wear sturdy runners or lightweight hiking boots. On wet days, rubber boots can be useful. If you are blister prone, experiment with different thicknesses of socks, or a combination of a thin inner sock and a thick outer sock.

Mountain weather can change rapidly. A sunny morning can become a wet, miserable afternoon, and vice versa. In addition, some of the trails are located in and alongside canyons, where cold, damp air prevails. If you plan to take one of the longer walks or hikes, carry a minimum of rain jacket and sweater as extra clothing. On hikes to higher elevations, take a warm hat and gloves as well. Your rain jacket can also be used as a windbreaker. Rainfall in the Rockies is usually very cold. You will need a full rainsuit and gloves on rainy days. An umbrella will suffice when showers are intermittent.

The effect of sunlight is intense at mountain elevations. Skin burns more rapidly because the atmosphere is thinner. Wind can also produce burns. Apply a good sunscreen on sunny days, and wear sunglasses and a light-coloured sun hat. Drink lots of water. Avoid beverages which contain caffeine, since these contribute to dehydration.

Use a day pack to carry clothing for several people, along with water bottle, snacks, sunscreen, insect repellent, and a small first-aid kit. The pack can be shared by different hikers. You will tire less easily if your camera, binoculars, or video unit are carried over the shoulder in a bag or on a strap, rather than in your hand. Because these trails receive heavy traffic, it is not wise to drink any water from trailside streams or lakes. Bring your drinking water with you from your hotel, home, or campground.

Rating the Walks and Hikes

The walks and hikes in this book follow maintained trails. None will present any difficulty to a fit pedestrian or seasoned walker. For the more casual walker, each walk and hike has been rated using the following system. Be sure to inquire about about trail conditions at park information centres before you begin.

Viewpoint: Less than 400 m to a viewpoint at roadside

Easy: Less than 1.6 kilometres (1 mile) and relatively flat

Moderate: 1.6-3.2 kilometres (1-2 miles) with noticeable elevation change (100-200 m)

Harder: More than 3.2 kilometres (2 miles), or shorter with considerable elevation change (200-400m)

Distances indicated are one way from trailhead to destination. The distance indicated for a loop trail is the total for the round trip. Wheelchair accessible trails and those recommended for families are listed on pages 149 and 150.

Trailhead elevations for these walks and hikes range between 1300 and 2350 m above sea level (4000 to 7700 ft). The effect of elevation may shorten your breath and create rapid fatigue. If you feel you have taken on more than you can endure, in terms of distance to be travelled or elevation to be gained, simply turn around and retrace your route to the trailhead.

"Lighting" indicates the optimum time for viewing the main attraction on the walk or hike on sunny days. However, mountain weather can produce spectacular lighting at any time. So, do not be discouraged if your schedule does not coincide with the recommended time.

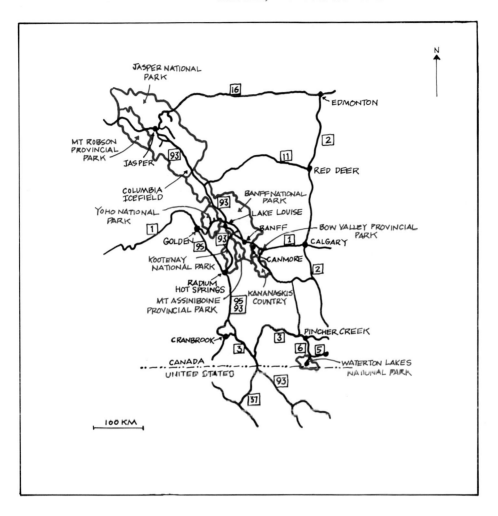

A Trail Etiquette

We each walk the trails of the Rocky Mountain parks for different reasons. Some of us do so for exercise, others to see the view. Still others are motivated by their interest in plants, birds, animals, or geology. Whatever our motivation, we must share the trails with each other. We must also tread lightly, so as not to damage what we have come to see.

The following trail etiquette respects the rights of others to an enjoyable hiking experience, and insures protection of the natural environment.

1. Pass each other without stepping off the trail. Avoid shortcutting on switchbacks. Do not walk around wet or snowy areas. In other words: *Please stay on the trail.* Walking off trail results in the trampling of surrounding vegetation and creates erosion problems. Twenty pairs of feet walking on untrammelled ground will create a permanent trail. At high elevations, it may take decades for damaged vegetation to recover.

2. Report any trail problems: chronic wet or muddy areas, broken steps or guard-rails, downed trees, slumps, washed-out bridges, etc. The staff at park information centres will record and act on this information.

3. Do not feed, entice, or harass wildlife. This is for your protection, as well as theirs. Report significant wildlife sightings to a park information centre.

4. Do not remove, deface, or disturb any natural or historical object – flower, tree, rock, fossil, dropped antler, etc. It is an offence to do so under the National Parks Act.

5. Use caution on trails shared with horses and bicycles. Cyclists should dismount to pass you. When you meet a horse party make verbal contact with the lead rider. Then quietly step to the *downhill* side of the trail. Do not speak or move until the last horse in the party is well past you.

6. Do not take your dog onto the trail.

7. Take all your litter back to the trailhead with you. Pick up any litter left by persons less considerate than yourself, and pack it out also. Recycle paper, plastic, glass, and cans. Deposit the remainder in the receptacles provided.

8. It is best not to smoke while using trails. Cigarette butts and used matches are among the most common types of litter. If you must smoke, pack out your cigarette butts.

9. Most of the major trails have outhouses at the trailhead. Please use them.

10. Do not enter a trail or area marked with a closed sign.

11. Interpretive brochures may be provided. Please return these if you do not wish to keep them.

12. Black and grizzly bears may be encountered throughout the Rockies. Read the pamphlet "You Are in Bear Country." Take extra care when a bear caution sign is posted for a particular trail or area.

BANFF AND THE BOW VALLEY

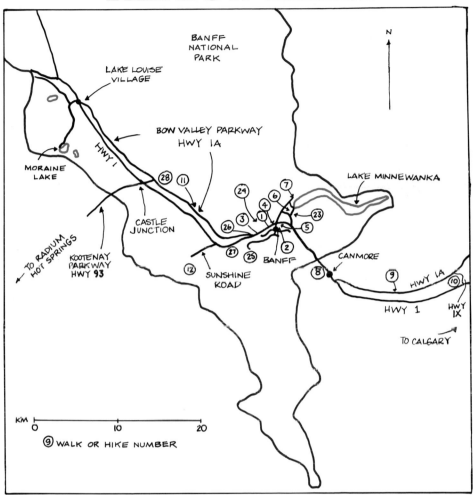

BANFF NATIONAL PARK

LAKE LOUISE VILLAGE

BOW VALLEY PARKWAY HWY 1A

HWY 1

MORAINE LAKE

LAKE MINNEWANKA

28 11

24 7

6

4

3 1

26 23

CASTLE JUNCTION

5

TO RADIUM HOT SPRINGS

KOOTENAY PARKWAY HWY 93

27 25

BANFF

2

CANMORE

12

8

SUNSHINE ROAD

9 HWY 1A

10

HWY 1 HWY IX

TO CALGARY

N

KM

0   10   20

9 WALK OR HIKE NUMBER

Banff, Canada's first national park, was founded in 1885 to preserve a small area near the Cave and Basin hot springs.

Most of the walks and easy hikes near Banff townsite are located in the Bow Valley, amid the grey limestone peaks of the front ranges. Two of the trails take you easily to mountain tops; one visits the largest alpine meadow system in the world; and others explore the extensive wetland areas immediately west of Banff townsite. Elk, bighorn sheep, mule deer, beaver, and black bear are the common large mammals you may see from these trails.

Short descriptions of other walks and easy hikes in Banff National Park are found on page 64.

1. **Bow Falls**

Photo above: Bow Falls has been eroded by the Bow River into a weakness in the underlying bedrock. The falls are reached by a pleasant walk along the Bow River from Banff townsite.

Trailhead: Banff townsite. Boat house at the corner of Wolf Street and Bow Avenue
Rating: moderate, 2.1km. Wheelchair accessible
Lighting: morning and early afternoon

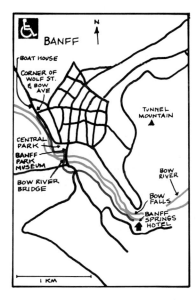

esidents of Banff are fortunate to have the Bow River in their downtown area. The walk along the riverbank to Bow Falls offers escape from the busy streets nearby and features tranquil views of this picturesque river. A visit to the Banff Park Museum in Central Park can be added to your walk to the falls.

The Bow is the longest river in Banff National Park. From its headwaters at Bow Lake, 90 km to the north, it drains an area of 2210 sq km. After flowing eastward through Banff, the Bow eventually joins the South Saskatchewan

River in southern Alberta. The river's name was suggested by Natives who made hunting bows from Douglas fir saplings found on its banks.

Severe flooding of the Bow in the vicinity of Banff townsite has been reported 11 times since 1894. The 1894 flood washed out the railway line and stranded guests at the Banff Springs Hotel. Stoney Natives from Morley were brought to Banff to entertain the idle tourists. This was the origin of the annual celebration of native culture known as Banff Indian Days.

The large coniferous trees along the riverbank and in Central Park are white spruce. Wetland areas undergo a fairly rapid process of succession, as swamp is transformed into forest. White spruce is the climax tree in this process, and mature stands indicate areas that were probably wetlands a few centuries ago.

The Bow River has not always followed this course through Banff. Before the last advance of the Wisconsin Glaciation, the river may have flowed to the north of Tunnel Mountain. When the glaciers receded 11,000 years ago, they blocked the river's course with moraines. A large lake formed west of the present townsite. Its waters eventually spilled through the gap between Tunnel Mountain and Mt. Rundle, at the present site of Bow Falls. The area west of Banff is still wetland – a legacy of the ancient lake.

Bow Falls have been eroded into a weakness in the bedrock where two rock formations meet. Looking upstream, the rocks of the left bank are 245 million years old, and those of the right bank are 320 million years old. The jagged formation of the left bank extends into the river bed, creating the rapids. Slightly downstream from the falls, the Spray River enters the Bow River. From here, you may ascend to the Banff Springs Hotel or return to your starting point.

Black-billed Magpie

A walk to Bow Falls is likely to include a sighting of the black-billed magpie. Its scientific name is *Pica*, which means "black and white" – an accurate description of its attractive plumage. The long tail feathers are highlighted with iridescent green.

Originally from Europe, the magpie is a large and vocal member of the crow family. It is found year-round in Banff. The magpie is not overly selective about what it eats; garbage is a favourite food. As with other members of the crow family, the magpie will also eat the young and eggs from other birdnests. Its diet is 60 percent meat. In recent years, magpies have developed a new food source – dead bugs on the front of vehicles. At the parking lot in Banff's Central Park you can watch magpies perched on car bumpers – their local bar and grill. The great horned owl is its principal predator. Magpies are known to mate for life and usually nest near water. Their homes are a bulging assembly of sticks, set in the crotch of a tree trunk.

2. **Tunnel Mountain**

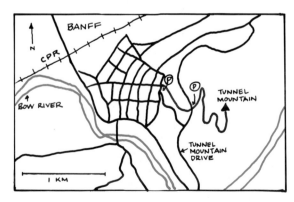

Photo above: The summit of Tunnel Mountain offers a paramount view of the Bow Valley near Banff townsite.

Trailhead: Parking area on the uphill side of St. Julien Road, 350 m south of Wolf Street. Easily accessible on foot from Banff townsite. Walk east on Wolf or Caribou streets.

Rating: harder, 1.8 km

Lighting: anytime

At an elevation of 1692 m (5550 ft), Tunnel Mountain is the lowest feature to which the name "mountain" is applied in the Rockies. Although it is a steep climb, ascending Tunnel Mountain along the well-beaten path hardly qualifies as mountaineering. From the summit, the hiker enjoys unrestricted views up and down Bow Valley.

In 1882, a surveyor for the Canadian Pacific Railway decided that Tunnel Mountain blocked the Bow Valley. He thought a tunnel would be required for the rails to proceed. A follow-up investigation found more than ample room for the railway in the valley between Tunnel and Cascade mountains. The tunnel was never built, but the name remains.

The trail climbs steadily on the southwest slope of Tunnel Mountain, crossing Tunnel Mountain Drive after 300 m. The forest here is lodgepole pine and Douglas fir. In the open spaces are bearberry, twinflower, common juniper, harebell, and brown-eyed Susans. Through the trees, there are fine views of the Banff Springs Hotel. The original hotel was constructed by the CPR in 1888. Most of the building we see today dates from 1928. The slopes behind the hotel rise to the ridge of Sulphur Mountain.

Tunnel Mountain is actually an extension of Mt. Rundle. The gap between the two was originally eroded by glaciers. Since then it has been enlarged by the Bow River. The mountain's shape is characteristic of one of the more common mountain types in the front ranges of the Rockies – the overthrust mountain. The steeply tilted slope that you have been climbing ends on a northeast-facing cliff. If you look across the gap to Mt. Rundle, you will see that it too is an overthrust mountain.

Looking east from Tunnel Mountain's summit, the mountains of the Fairholme Range are prominent. These mountains extend along the east side of the Bow Valley, from Lake Minnewanka to Exshaw. Mt. Rundle rises to the south. It was named for Methodist missionary Robert T. Rundle. In 1847, he preached to the Stoneys near the present site of the Banff airstrip. To the north is Cascade Mountain, highest summit in the vicinity of Banff. To the west, beyond the roof tops of Banff townsite, are the Vermilion wetlands. On the skyline are the peaks of the Massive Range. Given this view, you won't be surprised to learn that a fire lookout once occupied this spot.

Douglas Fir

The steep, sunny southwest-facing slopes of Tunnel Mountain are ideal habitat for the Douglas fir. In the Rockies, this tree does not reach the gigantic size of its coastal cousin. In typical form, it has a straight or gracefully curving trunk, and is 30 to 40 m tall.

Douglas firs are survivors. Their thick, furrowed bark allows them to withstand hot ground fires. Charring will often be visible on the bark of older trees. In the Rockies, where groundfires are common, most of the undergrowth will be removed, leaving a forest of widely spaced Douglas firs. Firs in such an environment may be 600 years old.

The Douglas fir is noted for its strength and is valued as commercial lumber and timber. Perhaps it is too valuable – by the year 2005, extensive old growth forests of this tree will be nonexistent outside protected areas, such as the national parks of the West.

3. **Marsh Trail**

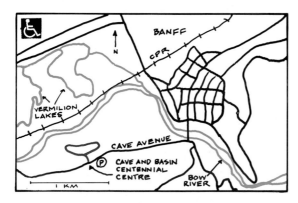

Trailhead: Follow Cave Avenue 1 km west of the Bow River bridge to the Cave and Basin centre. The trail begins at the west end of the pool.

Rating: easy, 500 m loop, boardwalk

Lighting: anytime

Of the 60 known hot springs in Canada, eight are near Banff townsite. Most of their combined outflow of more than 3800 litres per minute, eventually drains into the Vermilion wetlands, where the hot water changes the local environment. The Marsh Trail boardwalk loops from the Cave and Basin centre along the edge of this unique wetland, offering the opportunity to view plants and wildlife that are exotic to the Canadian Rockies. The area is a good one for bird-watching. A viewing blind is provided.

The hot water that emerges at Cave and Basin and other hot springs in the Banff area has not magically appeared from some underground water source. It all was originally surface water that managed to filter underground. The underground temperature typically increases 1°C for every 33 m descent into the earth's crust. At roughly 2.5 km below the surface, water reaches the boiling point and becomes pressurized. It naturally seeks crack systems to return to the earth's surface. Near Banff townsite, the water returns along the Sulphur Mountain Thrust Fault.

In its journey, the heated water dissolves minerals from the bedrock. A few minerals (uranium and radium) make the waters slightly radioactive. Some people think this is therapeutic. Sulphur dissolved in the water and sulphates metabolized by algae in the water combine to give the characteristic "rotten egg" smell. In mineral content, the hot springs at Banff are similar to those at Bath, England.

Since most of the rock in the area is limestone and dolomite, the hot spring waters carry calcium carbonate, a compound of lime, in solution. When gases in the water are released at the springs, this lime-rich solution precipitates as a crumbly rock known as tufa (TOO-fah). The tufa deposits in the Cave and Basin are 7 m thick.

The hot spring water prevents most of the wetland near Cave and Basin from freezing in winter. Some migratory birds remain all year: killdeer, snipe, American robin, and mallard duck. Six species of orchids bloom in spring on the banks above the wetlands, where the nonpoisonous wandering garter snake will also be found.

Minnows and sticklebacks are native to these warm wetland waters. Please remember that it is illegal to remove anything from a natural ecosystem in a national park, or to add anything.

Photo opposite: Hot spring water that seeps from the Cave and Basin springs has a moderating effect on the adjacent Vermilion wetlands. Along the Marsh Trail boardwalk you will see species of plants, fish, birds, and reptiles that are all exotic to the Rockies.

The Banff longnose dace is a minnow especially adapted to these warm waters. It lives nowhere else on earth. Even here it is now thought to be in danger of extinction. Competition from aquarium fish released in this marsh may have harmed its chances for survival.

Banff Longnose Dace

In the past, as many as eight species of fish have lived in the shallow, warm waters adjacent to the Marsh Trail. Of these, the only two native species were the Banff longnose dace and the brook stickleback.

A study in 1983 revealed that both native species were present. However, soon after, it was noted that their populations were in decline. It was feared that the more aggressive introduced species threatened the native fish with extinction. Sadly, in 1991, the Canadian Organization for the Status of Endangered Wildlife in Canada declared the Banff longnose dace extinct - a victim of human interference in a unique and protected ecosystem

4. **Fenland Trail**

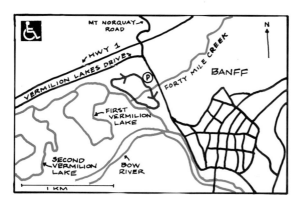

Trailhead: Follow Gopher Street north out of Banff. Cross the railway tracks. The trailhead is on the west side (left) of Gopher Street in

300 m. The trail may also be reached by walking north from the Bow Falls trailhead, corner of Wolf Street and Bow Avenue.

Rating: easy, 1.5 km loop. Wheelchair accessible. Brochure available at trailhead. Walk the loop clockwise.
Lighting: anytime

A fen is a lowland covered partially or entirely by water. The self-guiding Fenland Trail explores a shaded white spruce forest along the banks of Forty Mile Creek – an area typical of the wetlands west of Banff townsite. These wetlands are being transformed from open water to montane forest, in a process called succession.

The self-guiding brochure features ten interpretive stops:

1. The wetlands in the vicinity of Banff townsite were a natural barrier against fires which swept the Bow Valley after the arrival of the CPR in the 1880s. This mature

white spruce forest was spared by fire, and is ancient compared to most other forests in this valley.

2. Black bears are adept tree climbers. The scarred bark of trembling aspens reveals dark claw marks left by bears.

3. The view at this stop demonstrates how wetlands in the fen are shrinking, as the forest is becoming more extensive.

4. Many of the wetlands near Banff townsite have been created by beavers. The mound of sticks and mud is beaver lodge.

5. Beavers are aquatic rodents and create canals in their shallow ponds. The deeper canals provide escape routes from coyote, wolf, and bear.

6. Spring flood waters undermine the banks of Forty Mile Creek, causing trees to topple. At high water, disturbed soil washes into the nearby fen. This soil creates more habitat for vegetation, speeding up the transition from fen to forest.

7. The Vermilion wetlands are among the best bird-watching locations in the Rocky Mountain parks. Bald eagle, osprey, American dipper, red-winged blackbird, and a variety of waterfowl are among the common species.

8. Forty Mile Creek provides a natural moat, making the interior of the fen unattractive to predators. Cow elk raise their young here in spring, and bulls herd their harems during the autumn rut.

9. The buds of willows, aspen, and red osier dogwood are an important food source for elk, deer, and moose.

10. As the stumps reveal, the white spruce of this area made attractive building timber in Banff's early days. Hay crops were harvested from the nearby marshes until 1910. The level of the nearby First Vermilion Lake was controlled by a dam until the late 1970s. Such human impact is no longer tolerated in the vicinity of the fenland, as nature's balance is being restored.

Photo opposite: The Fenland Trail loops through a shaded forest along the banks of Forty Mile Creek and provides opportunity for viewing elk, beaver, deer, and songbirds.

Elk

The elk is the most plentiful large mammal in the Rocky Mountain parks. Estimates for Banff give a population of 3200 animals in summer and 1600 in winter. The adult bull elk stands 1.5 m tall at the shoulder. The coat is light brown, darker on the neck and legs, with a shaggy fringe on the underside of the neck. The animal is further identified by the tawny or white rump patch. Wapiti (WAH-pih-tee), the native name for elk, means "white rump."

Elk eat grasses, buds, and other tender vegetation. The males have antlers that can grow to a 1.8 m span. It is dangerous to approach elk during their autumn courtship or when a female is caring for young in the spring. The animals are very protective and will use their antlers and sharp hooves to attack a human intruder.

5. **Tunnel Mountain Hoodoos**

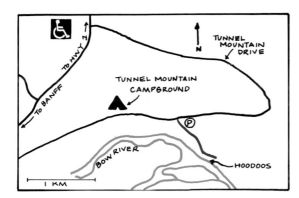

Photo above: The Tunnel Mountain Hoodoos have been sculpted by rainwater from thick deposits of glacial rubble.

Trailhead: 6 km east of Banff via Tunnel Mountain Drive. 1 km east of the entrance to Tunnel Mountain

Campground
Rating: easy, 500 m. Wheelchair accessible
Lighting: afternoon and evening

The paved Tunnel Mountain Hoodoos trail leads along the east bank of the Bow River to viewpoints overlooking the hoodoos and the Bow Valley. The trail also provides excellent views of Mt. Rundle and Tunnel Mountain.

Glaciers have shaped the Rockies. The ice rivers have ground down the landscape: sharpening the profile of the peaks, undercutting mountainsides, quarrying the bedrock, and producing masses of rock rubble known as till. During the Wisconsin Glaciation, an ice age which lasted from 75,000 to 11,000 years ago, there were three distinct advances of glacial ice from the high country of the Rockies toward the foothills. The first two advances extended beyond Banff carving the Bow Valley into its U-shape. When the ice receded, it left behind a blanket of rubble or till known as ground moraine, which in places is 70 metres thick.

As the Bow River eroded downward into the ground moraine, steep, gravelly banks of till were exposed. In much of the Rockies till contains a high percentage of calcium carbonate, the main compound used in making lime and cement. When mixed with water and compressed, calcium carbonate helps create a rock-like substance called tillite. Thus the exposed till banks along the Bow River are deceiving: they look like gravel, but they are as tough as concrete.

Over thousands of years, rainwater and intense spring runoff managed to erode furrows into the tillite banks near Tunnel Mountain Campground. These furrows were later enlarged until free-standing pillars of tillite developed. Called hoodoos, each of these pillars was originally protected by a capstone. Now missing their capstones, these hoodoos will eventually weather away until they collapse. Legends tell how natives thought the Tunnel Mountain Hoodoos were giants turned to stone, or teepees that housed "bad gods."

Douglas fir and whitebark pine grow along this trail. Whitebark pine has long, curved needles in bundles of five. Its trunk and branches are frequently contorted. The tree is locally common on cliff edges and in windy locations, such as this one.

Chinook Winds

The chinook (shih-NOOK) is a warm winter wind, which blows eastward at the mountain front. A native word that translates as "snow eater", chinook winds can raise temperatures as much as 40°C (72°F) in a few hours. The wind originates when warm air from a Pacific storm system meets a cold air mass situated east of the mountains. The storm system has shed most of its moisture on the western slopes of the Rockies, and the resulting dry air is heated as it sweeps down the eastern slope. Chinooks generally last from a few hours to a few days, but occasionally endure longer. There are roughly 20 chinook days a year in this area. Chinooks melt the snow, making the eastern valleys of the Rockies prime winter habitat for elk, deer, and bighorn sheep – and for their predators: wolf, coyote, and cougar.

6. **Bankhead**

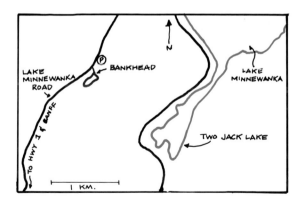

Trailhead: Follow Banff Avenue 3 km east from town to Highway 1. Keep straight ahead on the

Lake Minnewanka Road for 3.3 km. The trailhead is on the southeast (right) side of the road.

Rating: easy, 1.1 km loop. Brochure available at trailhead

Lighting: anytime

The Bankhead loop explores the industrial area of a coal mining community that flourished in the early 1900s. Artifacts associated with the mine are visible at trailside, and coal cinders are frequently underfoot.

Coal was discovered east of Banff, in 1885. The Canadian Anthracite Coal Company began mining at a location near the Canadian Pacific Railway main line the following year. Not wanting to depend on an outside supplier for its coal, the CPR obtained its own licences to mine coal in 1903.

Named after a Scottish town, the Bankhead mine was initially intended only to serve the railway's needs. However, the coal shortage of 1906-07 created a huge national demand for coal. The CPR expanded operations rapidly and built a townsite adjacent to the mine.

Mine production peaked in 1911; estimates vary from 250,000 to 416,000 tonnes of coal. The town's population also reached maximum the same year. Officially recorded as 900 persons, some reports indicate 2000 people lived at Bankhead. Most of the miners were immigrants: German, Italian, Swedish, Polish, and Chinese. The town featured a coal-burning power plant, which also supplied electricity to Banff.

Although resource extraction industries have been viewed as undesirable in national parks since 1930, park managers in the early 1900s encouraged mining at Bankhead. The park superintendent praised Bankhead in 1911: "With its beautiful homes and its teeming industrial life, it has already become a popular stopping place for tourists."

Bankhead's coal was extracted in an unusual fashion. Since the horizontal coal seams lay in the mountainside above the valley floor, the miners reached them by tunnelling upwards on a slight angle. Coal was then knocked downwards into railcars that gravity assisted in returning to the mine entrance. Three mining levels were developed. Over 300 kilometres of mining, transportation, and ventilation tunnels were excavated.

Bankhead's coal was high-quality semi-anthracite. However, 35 percent of the coal was little more than dust by the time it reached the mine portal. To salvage this coal, the CPR imported pitch from Pennsylvania, to manufacture coal briquettes. Despite the expense, the process proved successful.

As with most mining towns, Bankhead's history was one of boom and bust. An eight-month strike in 1912 began a decade-long economic slide, capped by a general miner's strike. As a result, the CPR closed the mine in 1922. Despite having produced more than 2.6 million tonnes of coal, the mine never re-opened, and Bankhead became a ghost town.

Photo opposite: In the early 1900s, the coal mining town of Bankhead flourished at the base of Cascade Mountain. The photograph shows the mine tipple, where the coal was sorted, circa 1906. Photograph by Elliott Barnes, courtesy of the Whyte Museum of the Canadian Rockies, Banff

Coal Train

Narrow-gauge trains transported coal from the mine to the tipple at Bankhead, where the coal was sorted. To prevent ignition of combustible gases in the mine tunnels, the trains were powered by compressed air. Known as "dinkys," the trains pulled 30 boxcars. Each could hold two tonnes of coal.

7. **Stewart Canyon**

Trailhead: Follow Banff Avenue 3 km east from town to Highway 1. Keep straight ahead on the Lake Minnewanka Road for 5.9 km to Lake Minnewanka. Park on the north (left) side of the road.
Rating: easy, 1.7 km
Lighting: anytime

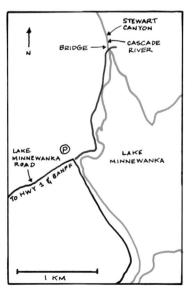

The Stewart Canyon trail is an ideal walk for families. It follows the north shore of Lake Minnewanka to a bridged canyon, where the Cascade River enters the lake. The pleasant, shaded trail leads through a mature lodgepole pine forest, with scattered Douglas fir. The parking lot area is the summer home for a flock of bighorn sheep.

With an area of 1295 hectares (3200 acres), Minnewanka is the largest lake in Banff National Park. The lake we see today is a hydroelectric reservoir. When the Bankhead mine developed nearby in 1903, it provided coal-fired electricity for its own needs, as well as those of Banff townsite. A miner's strike in 1912 temporarily disrupted Banff's electricity supply. A more reliable source was required, and a project to dam the outlet of Lake Minnewanka was conceived.

The initial dam raised the lake level 3 metres. In 1941, a much larger hydroelectric facility was constructed. The new dams raised the lake level a further 22 metres, submerging the village of Minnewanka Landing, and lengthening the lake by 8 km. The Ghost River at the lake's east end was also diverted into the lake.

Today, divers often explore the ruined village on the lake bottom.

Minnewanka means "lake of the water spirit." According to Stoney legend, the spirit in the lake is malevolent and belongs to a being – half fish, half human – that can move the lake waters at will. Earlier this century, Minnewanka was commonly referred to as Devil's Lake.

Stewart Canyon is known to geologists as a strike canyon. The Cascade River runs along a fault in the bedrock, where two thrust sheets meet. The canyon was named for George Stewart, who served as the first superintendent of Banff National Park.

Photo opposite: The trail to Stewart Canyon skirts the north shore of Lake Minnewanka, the largest body of water in Banff National Park. The lake is a hydroelectric reservoir. Dams have raised the natural lake level 25 m and added 8 km to its length.

Bighorn Sheep

The bighorn sheep is the symbol of Banff National Park and is the park's second most abundant large mammal. Many visitors confuse bighorn sheep with mountain goats. To simplify identification remember: sheep are light brown and goats are white.

The bighorn ram stands about a metre tall at the shoulder and, when mature, has a set of thick brown horns that spiral forward. These horns are never shed. Together with the skull they can make up 13 percent of the animal's weight. The dominant ram in the flock fights off challengers throughout the year by locking horns. If a slight scrap does not settle the matter, the two rams will rear up and charge headlong at each other. Armor bones beneath the horns prevent serious injury. But occasionally, duels to the death will take place. The horns of the female are much thinner and curve slightly backwards.

Bighorn sheep live in flocks of 10 to 50. Grasses are a prominent food in their diet. In winter, the animal's most important habitat is steep, south-facing slopes that remain relatively snow-free. Wolf, grizzly bear, and cougar are the main predators. Unfortunately, many flocks of sheep in the Rockies, including the one at Lake Minnewanka, have become habituated to humans and handouts of food. Please refrain from feeding them.

The beautiful blue and green waters of Grassi Lakes are the destination on this hike onto the lower flank of Mt. Rundle, west of Canmore. On the way to the lakes, the hiker obtains a spectacular view of the Bow Valley.

Trailhead: From Canmore, follow signs for the Canmore Nordic Centre. The Grassi Lakes turnoff is 1 km beyond the Nordic Centre, on the south (left).
Rating: harder, 1.75 km
Lighting: anytime

8. Grassi Lakes

The trail to Grassi Lakes climbs westward out of the Bow Valley towards Whiteman Gap – the pass between Chinaman's Peak and Mt. Rundle. The trail provides a spectacular view of the Canmore area. The beautiful blue and green waters of the lakes commemorate Lawrence Grassi, miner and trail builder. In the 1920s, Grassi and fellow workers from the nearby Georgetown coal mine built this trail to fill idle time during a strike. The trail features a rock staircase and formerly included a log ladder, to surmount a rock step. These devices were Grassi trademarks. He also used them on other trails in the Lake O'Hara area of Yoho National Park. Originally named Twin Lakes, the lakes were renamed in Grassi's honor in 1938. Grassi died in 1980, at the age of 90.

Initially the trail climbs gently through an open forest of lodgepole pine. The undergrowth includes the shrubs: buffaloberry, common juniper, Labrador tea, and prickly wild rose – Alberta's flower emblem. Adding splashes of colour are the wildflowers: ar-

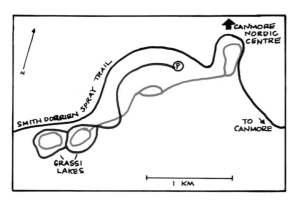

nica, harebell, twinflower, and western wood lily.

Soon, the trail climbs more steeply toward a 100 m waterfall that drains the lakes. Benches provide resting points. The interpretive signs at trailside describe the Spray hydroelectric project. The Spray River was dammed in the late 1940s and its waters were diverted east through Whiteman Gap into the Bow Valley. The signs neglect to mention a significant impact of this project: the area of the Spray development was formerly protected within Banff National Park, but it was removed in 1930 to allow the watercourse diversion and flooding to take place.

At the waterfall, the trail draws alongside the cliff edge for spectacular views of the limestone peaks of the Fairholme Range across the Bow Valley. The trail continues its climb.

Despite the many dams, reservoirs, and penstocks in this area, the Grassi Lakes are natural features of the landscape fed by water that seeps from the bedrock above. Fortunately, the lakes were spared during the hydroelectric development.

The beautiful colours of the lakes are characteristic of cold, clear water. Rocks on the lake bottoms are covered in dense blooms of algae. The American dipper (also called water ouzel) lives here. The dipper is the only aquatic songbird in North America. It stays in the mountains all year, feeding on larvae and insects in the water and rest

ing on rocks nearby. Its down-like feathers are coated with thick oil that repels water and helps keep the bird warm during winter.

The limestone cliffs above the lakes are remains of an ancient marine reef. It is thought the caves in these cliffs were used for shelter by Natives as recently as the late 1700s.

Western Wood Lily

The western wood lily is one of the prettiest wildflowers in the Rockies, and is locally common on grasslands and in pine forests at low elevation. The stem of this flower may be half a metre tall, and the flower as much as 10 cm across. The petals are deep orange, speckled inside with black dots on a yellow background. The flower blooms from early June until mid-July and is the floral emblem of Saskatchewan.

The western wood lily suffers a fate of many attractive plants. Its flower is commonly picked by admirers, and, like most wildflowers that grow from bulbs, the plant usually dies as a result. Please leave this beautiful flower for others to enjoy.

9. **Grotto Canyon**

Photo above: Grotto Canyon may be explored from within by walking off-trail along the stream bed. The canyon walls are 60 m high.

Trailhead: Grotto Mountain picnic area is on Highway 1A (12 km east of Canmore; 16 km west of the junction with Highway 1X).
Rating: harder, 2.5 km
Lighting: anytime

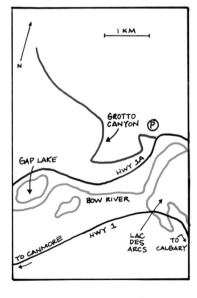

Although many walks in this book feature limestone canyons, Grotto Canyon is the only one that you can explore from within, by walking up a dry stream bed. This is also the only outing in this book that ventures off a maintained trail. Sturdy footwear is recommended.

The first 600 m of trail is along an old roadbed, carpeted with the tiny evergreen wildflower, yellow mountain avens. This plant is common in gravelly areas. Its nodding, yellow flowers are replaced in July by twisted seed pods which resemble those of dandelion.

The rocky rubble along the roadbed is material eroded from upstream in the canyon and deposited here by flash floods, creating a landform called an alluvial fan. The shape and height of this fan is prominent near the canyon mouth. Looking toward the Bow Valley, there is a view to Gap Lake, Mt. Lougheed, and Pigeon Mountain.

After turning north (right) toward the canyon, the hiker is greeted by a blast of cold air, chilled by the canyon walls. This is the end of well-defined trail. In the canyon you will be walking on water-worn rock slabs, rubble, and boulders.

Grotto Canyon is dry most of the time. How did the canyon become so deep, if so little water flows through it?

Evidence shows that the climate in this part of the world was quite warm from 8000 to 5000 years ago. The warmth caused glaciers on the upper mountainsides to melt rapidly. Water erodes limestone with relative ease. With a constant flow of water at high volume, most of the depth of this canyon could have been cut in a few thousand years.

Today, the erosional forces at work are frost-shattering in the cliffs. And during heavy rains, there are also flash floods of sedimentary debris.

In terms of the hiking experience, the confined atmosphere of Grotto Canyon is more typical of Utah than the Rockies. After walking about 1 km in the canyon, the canyon branches. The north (right) branch climbs to a small waterfall. The northwest (left) branch winds toward a more open valley, where limber pine and Douglas fir grow. In this valley there is a large hoodoo that contains a cave. Grotto means "cave," but the canyon does not take its name from this feature. Eugene Bourgeau, botanist with the Palliser Expedition, named the mountain west of the canyon in 1858, after a massive cavern in its slopes.

Grotto Canyon is popular with rock climbers. Their acrobatics may add some entertainment to your hike. In winter, waterfall ice climbers practice their craft on frozen seeps along the canyon walls.

Pictographs

Several panels of rock art can be found in Grotto Canyon. The illustrations are pictographs and were created with a paint that may contain ochre. The shaded locations of the pictographs have helped preserve them for perhaps 500 to 1000 years. Recently they have suffered heavily at the hands of careless visitors. For this reason, the author has chosen not to include their locations.

10. **Montane Trail**

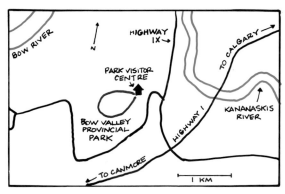

Trailhead: Follow Highway 1 to the junction with Highway 1X (80 km west of Calgary; 28 km east of Canmore). The Bow Valley Provincial Park Visitor Centre is 1 km north, on the west (left). The trail begins at the rear of the building.

Rating: easy, 2.2 km loop

Lighting: anytime

Bow Valley Provincial Park is located where the Rockies meet the prairies. As at Waterton Lakes National Park, the transition is marked by a tremendous variety of plant and animal life. The pockets of forest contain species native to the mountains, and the meadows contain flora and fauna commonly found on the prairies. Of the half dozen interpretive walks in the park, the Montane Trail, best displays this variety.

The montane ecoregion occupies valley bottoms in the Rockies. The climate is characterized by wind, extremes of temperature, and relatively low annual precipitation. The montane ecoregion provides important habitat for most larger mammals, especially in winter. Significant as it is, the montane makes up only 8 percent of the area in the Rocky Mountain parks. Most development in these parks has taken place in the montane, with severe impact on wildlife habitat.

On the Montane Trail you will see extensive evidence of the glacial past. During the Wisconsin Glaciation, an ice age which lasted from 75,000 to 11,000 years ago, massive rivers of ice, a thousand metres thick, flowed eastwards from the Rockies onto the plains. When they melted, the glaciers left behind many landforms made of boulders, sand, and gravel and created the undulating landscape of Bow Valley Provincial Park.

Winding ridges of gravel, called eskers, were formed by streams flowing beneath glacial ice. Part of the Montane Trail is along the crest of an esker. Cone-shaped piles of rubble called kames were deposited by meltwater flowing from the surface of the ice. Detached blocks of glacial ice melted into the rubble creating kettle ponds. Oval-shaped mounds called drumlins and other irregular clumps of moraine also dot the area.

The windiness at the mountain front is accentuated by winter chinooks (see page 21). The glacial landforms serve as windbreaks controlling the growth of forest. The windswept ridges have few trees. The protected hollows support groves of trembling aspen, white spruce, and lodgepole pine

The grassy meadows along the Montane Trail have been frequently burnt by hot ground fires. The fires eliminate tree growth and rejuvenate the grasses. The glacial landforms keep these fires localized, helping to sustain the mixture of forest and meadow. Wildlife such as elk and deer benefit by having open areas for grazing and forests for shelter.

Photo opposite: Mt. Yamnuska (yam-NUSS-kuh) is prominent from the half dozen interpretive trails in Bow Valley Provincial Park. Yamnuska means "flat-faced mountain."

McConnel Thrust Fault

Many who approach the Rockies from the east marvel at the front ranges, which rise dramatically, 1000 m above the foothills. During mountain building, forces in the earth's crust compressed the sedimentary rock formations until some buckled and broke. Then great sandwich layers of rock, called thrust sheets, slid upwards and northeast over the underlying rock layers. The boundary between the thrust sheet and the underlying rock layers is called a thrust fault.

The McConnel thrust fault area, the most easterly thrust fault in the front ranges, can be seen from Bow Valley Provincial Park at the base of Mt. Yamnuska. Here, layers of limestone 540 million years old have been thrust upwards and over, undisturbed shale that is 90 million years old. This massive thrust sheet of limestone slid 16 kilometres.

Limestone is much more resistant to erosion than shale. Hence the cliff of Yamnuska has endured, while the exposed shales of the adjacent foothills have weathered away, creating the exaggerated vertical relief at the mountain front

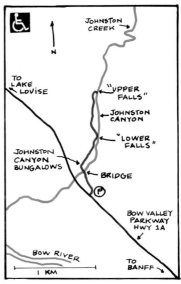

11. **Johnston Canyon**

Photo above: The lower falls in Johnston Canyon mark a point where Johnston Creek has encountered a resistant layer of dolomite in the limestone bedrock. The falls are reached by a walkway suspended within the canyon.

Trailhead: Bow Valley Parkway (Highway 1A), 23.6 km west of Banff; 6.5 km east of Castle Junction

Rating: lower falls, easy, 1.1 km; upper falls, moderate, 2.7 km

Lighting: early afternoon

O f the seven trails in this book that lead to limestone canyons, the Johnston Canyon Trail provides a unique perspective. An ingenious suspended walkway takes you into the heart of the canyon. The walkway provides close-up views of waterfalls and the effects of flowing water.

Johnston Creek has not always flowed through this canyon. At the end of the Wisconsin Glaciation, 11,000 years ago, the creek flowed east of here alongside Mt. Ishbel, and it emptied down-valley into the Bow River. About 8000 years ago, a massive landslide broke free from Mt. Ishbel. The Hillsdale Slide blocked the course of Johnston Creek, forcing it to seek another outlet. Eventually the creek took advantage of a weakness in the bedrock, a fault surface, and eroded the canyon.

There are seven waterfalls in Johnston Canyon. Each marks the location of a relatively resistant outcrop of dolomite in the limestone bedrock. The dolomite lip of a waterfall indures while the limestone beneath is eroded into a plunge pool, by the incessant pounding of the water. Eventually, the lip is greatly undercut by the plunge pool and collapses. The falls then migrate slightly upstream. The highest waterfall and deepest point in Johnston Canyon is the 30 m upper falls.

Limestone erodes relatively easily in water because rainfall and runoff are naturally slightly acidic. This chemical erosion, coupled with abrasion by sediments in the water and frost shattering of the canyon walls, has created interesting formations in the canyon. One of these is a natural tunnel at the lower falls. As with other limestone canyons in the Rockies, Johnston Canyon exhibits potholes and abandoned channels. There is even an abandoned waterfall.

In the canyon, lodgepole pine and a few Douglas fir trees grow on south-facing slopes, while the colder and wetter north-facing slopes support spruce and fir. Red squirrel, American dipper, porcupine, black swift, and common raven are residents of the canyon, and mule deer will sometimes be seen near the parking lot. The canyon was named for one of the prospectors from nearby Silver City, a mining boomtown in 1884, that no longer exists.

Travertine

Travertine (TRAH-vur-teen) is a banded limy rock created mainly by chemical action. However, it is remarkable that the least complex of the lifeforms on earth, algae, can be biological agents in the formation of travertine. The algae remove carbon dioxide from water during photosynthesis and deposit a film of calcium carbonate as a waste product. The calcium carbonate eventually builds up into banded limestone. A similar process took place in ancient seas hundreds of millions of years ago.

Small travertine deposits occur in many canyons in the Rockies, but the travertine wall at the Upper Falls in Johnston Canyon is the most extensive. There are 25 species of algae here. The formation of travertine is assisted by the spray from the waterfall, and by spring water from several outlets on the canyon wall. If you look at the base of the wall, you will see that this accumulation of travertine is quite thick and overhangs the creek.

12. **Sunshine Meadows**

The trail to Rock Isle Lake is the most popular excursion at Sunshine Meadows. From the upper gondola terminal, walk uphill (south) on a broad trail. Fifteen metres past the avalanche station take the narrow trail branching to the east (left). This trail ascends gradually through the sparse treeline forest. Flower-filled meadows and vistas of rolling terrain dotted with lakes await the hiker in the alpine garden above.

Sunshine Meadows occupy a 14 kilometre arc along the Continental Divide, at an average elevation of 2225 m (7300ft). The average annual temperature is -4°C, and more than three quarters of the precipitation falls as snow – seven metres annually. In most years, snowbanks linger well into July. Despite the climate, hardy wildflowers bloom between mid-July and mid-August.

Many of the trees on Sunshine Meadows are in stunted krummholz form. In the shelter of the tree islands, snowbanks linger, providing good habitat for moisture-loving wildflowers such as the glacier lily and bracted lousewort.

One of the most common flowers in the Sunshine Meadows is the western anemone (an-EMM-owe-nee) of the buttercup family. The large creamy white flowers bloom briefly and are not seen by many visitors. However, the showy greenish seedhead remains until autumn, making the plant attractive to photographers.

After the trail levels off, it crosses the Continental Divide, the boundary between Banff National Park, Alberta and Mt. Assiniboine (a-SINNI-boyne) Provincial Park, B.C. Mt. Assiniboine is the sixth highest mountain in the Rockies, and the highest south of the Columbia Icefield. On clear days, it is visible 20 km to the south.

Keep right at the trail junctions, and you will soon reach Rock Isle Lake. The viewing platform makes a convenient turnaround point for many hikers. However, it is possible to extend this outing by climbing up a trail to another viewing platform on the crest of Standish Ridge, immediately north of the lake (800 m), or by proceeding to Grizzly and Larix lakes (3.7 km loop).

Summer gondola access to Sunshine Village has been provided for visitors since 1984. More than 30,000 hikers now visit these meadows each summer. In an attempt to lessen the harm done by such a large number of visitors, trails have been hardened with gravel. The gravel has been helicoptered here at great expense. Please keep to the well-built trails in order to spare the surrounding vegetation.

Photo opposite: Sunshine Meadows is part of an extensive alpine meadow system. Rock Isle Lake is an alluring destination, reached by hiking across a flower-filled tundra.

An Alpine Garden

The vegetation community at Sunshine Meadows is known to botanists as heath tundra. It consists of mountain heather, everlasting, fleabane, valerian, arctic willow, and sedges. In addition, 340 other vascular plant species have been found here above treeline. This represents more than one-third of the species in Banff and Jasper national parks. Most of these plants are perennial. Some are rare, and many are near the extreme northern or extreme southern limits of their ranges.

LAKE LOUISE TO COLUMBIA ICEFIELD

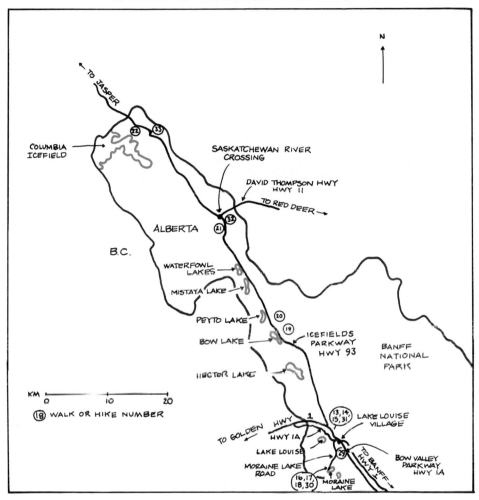

Photos opposite, left to right, top to bottom: Calypso orchid (Venus slipper), glacier lily (dogtooth violet), red-flowered (western) columbine, queen's cup, Indian paintbrush, moss campion.

The walks and easy hikes between Lake Louise and Columbia Icefield feature the trademark views of the Canadian Rockies: glacier-capped peaks, flower-filled meadows, and blue-green glacial lakes. Wildlife is often seen along the Icefields Parkway, which provides access to many of the trailheads.

Many of these trails are snow-covered for much of the year. If you are visiting early or late in the summer, please check trail conditions at the park information centre in Lake Louise.

The ice-draped flank of Mt. Victoria provides the backdrop for the world-renowned view at Lake Louise.

Trailhead: From Lake Louise Village, follow Lake Louise Drive 5.5 km to the public parking lots at the lake. Paved walkways lead to the lakeshore.
Rating: moderate, 1.9 km. Wheelchair accessible
Lighting: sunrise and morning

13. Lake Louise Shoreline

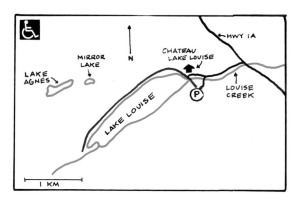

The paved shoreline trail in front of Chateau Lake Louise probably sees more foot and wheelchair traffic annually than any other place in the Rockies, except Banff Avenue. The view of Mt. Victoria reflected in the lake is one of the classic views in the mountain world.

In 1882, pioneer guide and outfitter Tom Wilson was led to Lake Louise by a Stoney Native. The Stoneys called it Lake of the Little Fishes. Wilson called it Emerald Lake. Two years later, the name was changed to Lake Louise, to honor the fourth daughter of Queen Victoria.

Wilson's visit brought the lake to the attention of the Canadian Pacific Railway. In 1890, the company constructed the first chalet at the lake, and began to advertise its rustic shelter to clients who were well-heeled and willing to rough it a little. From this building, which housed fewer than a dozen guests, the chalet went through continual transformation yielding the 515 room Chateau Lake Louise a century later.

Lake Louise occupies a glacially carved valley adjacent to the Continental Divide. The lake is 2.4 km long, roughly 500 m wide, and 90 m deep. Its elevation is 1731 m, slightly more than a mile above sea level. The surrounding mountains shade its waters for much of the year, and the lake's surface is frozen from November until June. The maximum water temperature, 4°C (39°F), is reached in early August. Clearly, the swimming is not the attraction here!

What is so alluring about Lake Louise is the symmetry of the scene. Mt. Victoria, 10 km distant, and its reflection are framed perfectly by the converging lines of cliffs and slopes at the far end of the lake. At least one world traveller has ranked "Lake Louise at sunrise" in the top ten of the world's natural wonders.

A developed trail exists along the northwest edge of the lake only (viewer's right). This gravelled trail eventually leads to the Plain of Six Glaciers, but those looking for a shorter outing will find the boat landing or the delta at the far end of the lake make good places to turn around.

Interpretive panels, describing elements of the human and natural history of Lake Louise, can be viewed on the south side of the bridge at the lake's outlet and along the boardwalk to the boathouse. A plaque commemorating the designation of the four mountain parks as a World Heritage Site was unveiled by the Duke of Edinburgh during a royal visit in 1985.

The Subalpine Forest

The forest adjacent to Chateau Lake Louise has been greatly altered during the last century. However, just a short walk away from the Chateau, you enter undisturbed subalpine forest that is centuries old. The most common trees in this forest are Engelmann spruce and subalpine fir, whose branches are draped with tree lichens. The smooth, silvery bark of the subalpine fir is often covered in resin blisters, which give the forest its sweet fragrance. A carpet of rootless plants called feather mosses thrives on the damp forest floor, along with the flowers dwarf dogwood and arnica.

The subalpine forest is frequently called "the snow forest." More than 4 m of snow falls here each year. Common wildlife includes the masked shrew, pack rat, least chipmunk, red squirrel, American marten, snowshoe hare, beaver, lynx, wolverine, porcupine, great horned owl, spruce grouse, Clark's nutcracker, and gray jay.

14. **Plain of Six Glaciers**

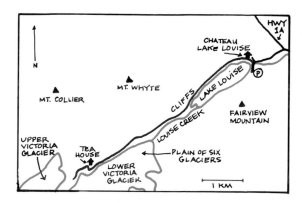

Trailhead: From Lake Louise Village, follow Lake Louise Drive 5.5 km to the public parking lots at the lake. Paved walkways lead to the lakeshore.
Rating: harder, 5.3 km
Lighting: morning

The hike to the Plain of Six Glaciers is a continuation of the Lake Louise walk and delivers the hiker to the jumble of ice and rock below Mt. Victoria. It is the longest outing in this book and also one of the most popular. There is a teahouse at the end of the walk. Hikers should have sturdy footwear and be prepared for changeable weather.

At the far end of Lake Louise, the trail passes beneath hundred-metre cliffs, which are popular with rock climbers. The rock is colourful Gog quartzite. It underlies most of the mountains in the area. The trail rounds the cliffs and draws alongside the delta at the lake's inlet. Beaver are sometimes seen here in the morning and early evening.

Most of the elevation on this hike is gained in two short climbs. The first of these takes you through subalpine forest, and across the openings created by several large avalanche paths on the lower slopes of Mt. Whyte. In the valley bottom to the south (left), is a jumble of grey boulders – rockslide debris known as "The Bear's Den." Farther up the valley, the trail traverses a low cliff edge. Use care here if the rock is wet. If the exposure of the traverse is not to your liking, you can by-pass this section by dropping to the moraine on your left.

The "plain" is a 1 km long, gravel outwash area adjacent to the Lower Victoria Glacier. From it, six glaciers are visible: Lower Victoria, Upper Victoria, Aberdeen, Lefroy, Upper Lefroy, and Popes. (A seventh glacier, which does not flow into this valley, is also visible on the north peak of Mt. Victoria.). During the Wisconsin Glaciation, the combined flow of the six glaciers carved the valley containing Lake Louise. Since then, the ice has shrunk greatly in length and mass. Lower Victoria Glacier has receded 1220 metres in the last 160 years.

The trail switchbacks just before the teahouse is reached. Look for mountain goats and porcupines in the vicinity. The Plain of Six Glaciers teahouse is at 2135 m

(7005 ft) and was constructed in 1924 by Swiss guides employed by the CPR. The teahouse was to serve as a hiker's destination and a staging point for mountaineers. Today, lunch, refreshments, and snacks are available in season. Overnight accommodation is no longer offered.

Those with sturdy footwear and warm clothing can extend this hike up the valley, 1.6 km beyond the teahouse. There is a spectacular viewpoint on the moraine overlooking the Lower Victoria Glacier.

Glacier Types

Glacial ice forms, in areas where more snow accumulates annually than melts. The shape of a glacier depends on its location and features of the surrounding landscape. Icefields form on relatively flat areas at high elevations. Outlet valley glaciers flow from icefields into the valleys below. Alpine valley glaciers occupy high mountain valleys and are not fed by icefields. Cirque glaciers occupy and erode bowl-shaped depressions in mountainsides. Niche glaciers form at high elevations, where indentations in a mountainside trap windblown snow. Any of these glacier types can also be called a hanging glacier if the ice terminates on a cliff. With the exception of icefields and outlet valley glaciers, all of these glacier types can be seen during the Plain of Six Glaciers hike.

15. **Lake Agnes**

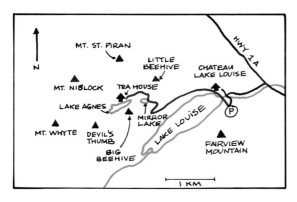

Lake Agnes is a glacial tarn, nestled in a cirque valley high above Lake Louise. The steep hike to the lake is one of the most popular in the Canadian Rockies. The lake is walled-in by ragged cliffs; a striking contrast to the open prospect northeastward across the Bow Valley.

Trailhead: From Lake Louise Village, follow Lake Louise Drive 5.5 km to the parking lots at the lake. Paved walkways lead to the lakeshore. Walk along the lakeshore to the trail junction on the far side of the Chateau. The trail to Lake Agnes branches uphill to the right. **Rating**: harder, 3.4 km **Lighting**: morning

The Native guide who led Tom Wilson to Lake Louise in 1882, told him of two other lakes on a nearby mountainside. "The goat's looking glass" was a small lake where goats combed their beards and studied their reflections in the tranquil waters. Further above was another lake, subsequently named Agnes after the wife of Canada's first prime minister.

The lakes soon became known as "the lakes in the clouds." One of the first tasks of Willoughby Astley, manager of Chalet Lake Louise, was cutting a trail to reach them. Today, many visitors are soon humbled by the unrelenting climb that resulted from Astley's work, and also by the effect of the elevation. Take it easy on this hike, and allow a half day for the round trip.

The first two kilometres of the trail to Lake Agnes are through dense subalpine forest, in which the most common trees are Engelmann spruce and subalpine fir. Tree branches are draped with tree lichens, and feather mosses cover the damp forest floor. At km 1.6, the trail makes a 180 degree switchback turn on a narrow avalanche path. The beautiful waters of Lake Louise are visible below, as is the delta at the lake inlet. The massive quartzite cliffs across the lake form the lower flanks of Fairview Mountain. At this point, you are slightly less than halfway to your destination – both in distance and elevation to be gained.

After the next prominent turn, the forest becomes thinner, marking the transition to the upper subalpine ecoregion. The trail crosses a metre wide cut-line in the forest that formerly contained a wooden pipeline. Until 1984, Lake Agnes was the water supply for the Chateau. A section of pipeline is still imbedded in the trail.

At the wooden horse/hiker barrier, turn left. From here to Lake Agnes, the trail is shared with horse traffic. In a few minutes, you reach "the goat's looking glass" (Mirror Lake). The quartzite buttress of Big Beehive forms the lake's backdrop. Although mountain goats now prefer to avoid this busy area, the mountainsides nearby are still home to from 50 to 60 of these animals.

Golden-mantled Ground Squirrel

The golden-mantled ground squirrel is one of the most common small mammals in the Rockies, with a body about 20 cm long. Its coat is light grey on top, cream underneath, and reddish brown on the head and shoulders. The black tail is about 10 cm long. Two white stripes bordered with black extend from the shoulders to the rear legs. The eye is circled with white. The only other animal in the Rockies that looks like this is the least chipmunk, which is about two-thirds the size. The chipmunk has four greyish white stripes that extend from the nose to the rear legs.

Like most rodents, the golden-mantled ground squirrel appears hyperactive to us. It flits about the forest floor gathering leaves, seeds, flowers, and fungi. Unfortunately, at the teahouse, it also has the habit of jumping onto tables and eating unattended muffins. It will dunk its head in a pitcher of milk for a drink. Though amusing, this behaviour is ultimately harmful. It is also not in the best interest of unsuspecting humans, who may take a bite of banana bread after one of these flea-infested critters has left its tracks in the butter. Please be responsible with your food and keep it away from the wildlife.

Golden-mantled ground squirrels spend the months of September to May in semi-hibernation, rousing every few days to nibble on foods stashed in their burrows.

The steep hike to Lake Agnes is one of the most popular in the Rockies. The lake is named for the wife of Canada's first Prime Minister. A teahouse operates on the lakeshore during the summer months.

avalanche path, the glaciated peaks of Mt. Aberdeen and Mt. Temple are visible. Mt. Temple is the highest peak in the vicinity of Lake Louise, and third highest in Banff National Park.

The final approach to Lake Agnes is made by two flights of stairs, leading to the teahouse on the lakeshore. Many hikers arrive breathless after the climb. The elevation of Lake Agnes is 2038 m (6685 ft). Since leaving the Chateau, you will have gained over 300 m, roughly equivalent to climbing the stairs to the top of a 100 storey building.

Walter Wilcox, one of the first explorers in the Lake Louise area, called Lake Agnes "a wild tarn imprisoned by cheerless cliffs." Despite the many visitors today, his description of Lake Agnes still holds merit. It is also technically accurate. Lake Agnes is a glacial tarn occupying a cirque. The glacier which created it has long since disappeared. But at perhaps no other location in the Rockies is the amphitheatre-like form of a cirque so evident.

The main trail to Lake Agnes continues to the north (right) from Mirror Lake. Soon you enter an opening in the forest. This is the base of a kilometre long avalanche path on Mt. St. Piran (pih-RAN). Avalanches of snow sweep this section of the mountain annually. If you look downhill from the trail, you will see a jumble of dead trees and branches – testimony to the power of moving snow. Mt. St. Piran was named for the English birthplace of the original chalet manager, Willoughby Astley. Looking south from high on the

From the lakeshore near the teahouse, the mountains forming the lake's backdrop are, from left to right: Big Beehive, Devil's Thumb, Mt. Whyte, Mt. Niblock, and Mt. St. Piran. Sir William Whyte was second vice-president of the CPR, and John Niblock was a superintendent of the railway in the mountain region. Lake Agnes was one of their favourite fishing holes. Fishing is not allowed in the lake today.

Earlier this century, the CPR constructed three teahouses in the Lake Louise area, in order to encourage use of the trails. The Lake Agnes teahouse was the first of these, and is believed to have been built in 1901. The present building is privately owned, and reconstruction was completed in 1981. Lunch, refreshments, and snacks are available in season, from mid-June to early October. Inquire at the park information centre if you are hiking in the off season.

Many rodents inhabit the vicinity of the teahouse: Columbian ground squirrel, red squirrel, least chipmunk, and golden-mantled ground squirrel. The hoary marmot and the pika, a member of the rabbit family, live in the boulder fields along the lakeshore. The sky over the teahouse is busy with the comings and goings of Clark's nutcrackers and gray jays. While it is tempting to feed these birds and mammals, please refrain from doing so.

If you think the trail to Lake Agnes is steep, imagine what the downhill trip would be like wearing a pair of cross-country skis! The wild run down from the teahouse is a favourite with local skiers in winter.

Clark's Nutcracker and Gray Jay

The Clark's nutcracker is the more numerous of the two common birds at Lake Agnes. Its plumage is medium gray on the body, with attractive black and white flashes on the wings. The long, black beak is designed for extracting the seeds from pine cones, and for burrowing into rotten wood to extract ants and larvae. Berries make up the rest of its diet. A member of the crow family, the bird was named for Captain William Clark of the Lewis and Clark Expedition.

If you've made the mistake of enticing one of these birds with a crumb or two, the welcome will soon wear off. The Clark's nutcracker has poor table manners and will, quickly and loudly, announce your vulnerability to a host of its cohorts. Soon you will have a convention of nutcrackers on your plate. Please allow these birds to fend for themselves in the forest nearby.

The other common grey, black, and white bird you will see at Lake Agnes is the gray jay, also known as the whiskey-jack. It is smaller and quieter than the Clark's nutcracker, and it has a smokier coloured coat, a short blunt beak, and a white forehead.

16. **Moraine Lake Rockpile**

Trailhead: From Lake Louise Village, follow Lake Louise Drive 3 km to the Moraine Lake Road. Turn south (left). Follow this road 12 km to its end at Moraine Lake. The trailhead is at the southeast corner of the parking lot.
Rating: easy, 250 m
Lighting: morning

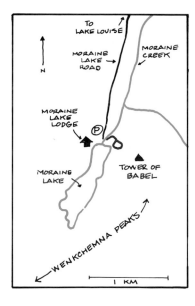

The best view at Moraine Lake is obtained from the top of this rockpile at its outlet. From the parking lot cross the bridge over the outlet stream, and follow the interpretive trail to the top of this knoll. The colour of the lake is accentuated from this viewpoint, and the Wenkchemna Peaks stand in solemn splendour, an icy wall along the south side of the valley.

When American explorer Walter Wilcox made the first visit to Moraine Lake in 1899, he assumed the lake was dammed by a glacial moraine. The name "Rockslide Lake" would have been more accurate. The rubble pile at the lake's outlet is probably the debris from one or more rockslides.

Most of the blocks in the rockpile are quartzite, a kind of sandstone known locally as the Gog Formation. This sedimentary rock is made of particles deposited on the floor of a shallow inland sea between 570 and 540 million years ago. The Gog quartzite is one of the hardest and most common rocks in the Rockies. In some areas the formation is 4 kilometres thick.

Rockslides are often home to the tiny pika of the rabbit family, and the rodents: least chipmunk, golden-mantled ground squirrel, and hoary marmot. The crevices between the boulders make natural denning and food storage sites for these animals.

Moraine Lake is fed by waters from Wenkchemna Glacier, whose rubble-covered surface is concealed from view at the far end of the lake. Wenkchemna is the Stoney word meaning "ten." Explorer Samuel Allen named many of the peaks in the valley in 1894, using the Stoney words for the numbers one to ten. The valley became known as the Valley of the Ten Peaks. In 1979, the name Wenkchemna Peaks was officially adopted.

Today, only peaks number four, nine, and ten – Tonsa, Neptuak, and Wenkchemna – retain their original Stoney names. Five of the peaks have been named for mountaineers (Fay, Little, Perren, Allen, Tuzo); one for its physical appearance (Deltaform); and another for an Alberta politician (Bowlen). The Wenkchemna Peaks have been featured on the Canadian twenty dollar bill since 1969.

Photo opposite: The Wenkchemna Peaks form a stunning backdrop in this view from the rockpile at Moraine Lake.

Ripple Rock

It is difficult for most of us to comprehend that the massive Rockies were created from sediments deposited in ancient seas. In a few locations graphic evidence of their marine origin has been recorded in the rock.

As you ascend the staircase to the rockpile, you will notice a prominent example of ripple rock. Anyone who has spent time at a beach knows that beach sand frequently takes on a rippled effect from the constant action of wavelets. Here, preserved in rock 560 million years old, is an indication that the same process was at work before the Rockies were uplifted. Geologists know that this kind of rippling takes place only in shallow water. So, they can roughly describe the environment where the original sediments were deposited.

Since this example of ripple rock was brought to public attention, it has been heavily damaged. Sedimentary rock of this type is very fragile. Please do not touch.

17. **Lower Consolation Lake**

Trailhead: From Lake Louise Village, follow Lake Louise Drive 3 km to the Moraine Lake Road. Turn south (left). Follow this road 12 km to its end at Moraine Lake. The trailhead, shared with Moraine Lake Rockpile, is at the southeast corner of the parking lot.
Rating: moderate, 2.9 km
Lighting: early morning, late afternoon

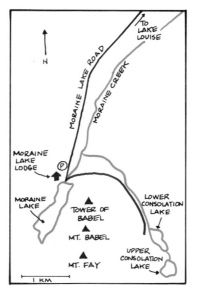

Explorer Walter Wilcox described the view at Lower Consolation Lake as "one of the most beautiful pictures I have ever seen in the Rockies". After his visit to Moraine Lake in 1899, Wilcox made a side trip to Consolation Lakes. To Wilcox, the Moraine Lake area had appeared sombre enough to merit the name Desolation Valley. In contrast, the valley into which this trail leads was perceived more favourably. Thus the Consolation Valley and its lakes were named.

The trail to Lower Consolation Lake contours around the base of the Moraine Lake Rockpile and passes through a quartzite boulder field. Here, you are walking on a natural rock causeway across the outlet of Moraine Lake. For the next two kilometres, the trail climbs gradually through subalpine forest and swings southeast into the hanging valley that contains Consolation Lakes. At km 1.6, the Taylor Lake trail branches north (left). Here the forest floor is carpeted with grouseberry, and spruce grouse may be seen.

For the last 500 m to the outlet of the lower lake, the trail borders a subalpine wet meadow. This meadow is a frost hollow. Cold air collects here and stunts vegetation, so that trees will not grow. Elephant head, fleabane, bracted lousewort, and the colourful Indian paintbrush are among the flowers that you will see here.

The trail ends near the shore of the lower lake. At the far end of the valley, the glacier-draped crags of Mt. Bident ("two teeth") and Quadra Mountain ("four summits") thrust toward the sky. The larch-covered slopes of Panorama Ridge flank the east side of the valley, and on the west are the colossal cliffs of Mt. Babel and Mt. Fay. In the foreground are the lichen-covered quartzite blocks that dam the placid waters of Lower Consolation Lake.

The Consolation Lakes are tarns, occupying depressions gouged out of the bedrock by glaciers. The Upper Consolation Lake is slightly higher and concealed from view, a kilometre of rough and wet boulder-hopping, up-valley.

Photo opposite: The ragged, glaciated crests of Mt. Bident and Quadra Mountain are reflected in Lower Consolation Lake shortly after sunrise.

Rock Lichens

Colourful rock lichens (LIKE-enz) are rootless, leafless plants made up of fungi and algae. The fungi protect the algae; and the algae in turn produce food for the fungi. The byproduct of this relationship is humic acid, which accelerates the chemical breakdown of rock and the formation of primitive soil. Rock lichens grow in colonies, radiating outwards in a circular fashion at an incredibly slow though consistent rate. It is thought some rock lichen colonies may have begun life at

the end of the Wisconsin Glaciation, 11,000 years ago! Please try to avoid walking on them if you hop across the boulders.

Two common rock lichens in the Rockies are the orange *Xanthoria* (zan-THOR-ee-uh), and the green and black map lichen (photo). Lichens were formerly widely used in the creation of dies. Litmus, a substance derived from lichens, is today used in the manufacture of litmus paper. Lichens grow well only in unpolluted environments, and their presence is an indication that air and water quality are being maintained.

18. **Larch Valley**

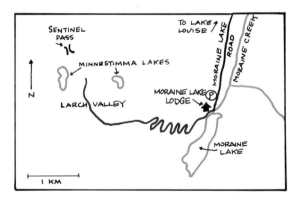

Trailhead: From Lake Louise Village, follow Lake Louise Drive 3 km to the Moraine Lake Road. Turn south (left).

Follow this road 12 km to its end at Moraine Lake. The trail begins on the lakeshore in front of the lodge.

Rating: harder, 3.2 km

Lighting: anytime

The trail to Larch Valley branches west (right) from the shore of Moraine Lake, just beyond the lodge. In the next 2.4 km, the trail gains 400 m of elevation, making it one of the steepest excursions in this book. The hiker's reward is splendid views of the Wenkchemna Peaks, and the opportunity to walk in a forest of Lyall's larch.

The first kilometre of steady uphill prepares you for the really hard work on this hike – ten switchbacks (one for each of the ten peaks?) – that deliver you to the mouth of Larch Valley. There is a tendency when on a steep trail to hike with your head down. Take time on this hike to stop and look around. You will notice a gradual transition from subalpine to upper subalpine forest as you gain elevation. Moraine Lake can be seen through the trees below.

The Larch Valley trail branches north (right) at the top of the switchbacks. From here, the trail climbs gradually through a treeline forest of Lyall's larch. Beyond the footbridge, there is a pronounced opening in the forest. This meadow is a frost hollow. If you look closely at the trees on the edge of the adjacent forest, you will see frost has stunted the growth of the tree branches. The meadow is home to a colony of Columbian ground squirrels. The small mounds have not resulted from their burrowing. They are frost hummocks, unusual soil features created by repeated freezing and thawing of the soil.

Above the treetops, the sweeping vista of the Wenkchemna Peaks is revealed. Explorer Samuel Allen named these mountains in 1894, using Stoney words for the numbers from one to ten. He assumed there were ten peaks in the valley. In reality, there are eighteen. From east (left) to west (right), the peaks in view are today named: Mt. Babel, Mt. Fay (with the prominent glaciers), Mt. Bowlen, "Peak 3 1/2", Tonsa, Mt. Perren, Mt. Allen, Mt. Tuzo, Deltaform Mountain, and Neptuak Mountain. Mt. Little ("Peak 2") is concealed behind Mt. Bowlen.

The trail resumes its climb and soon passes treeline. Ahead lies the approach to Sentinel Pass, the highest point reached by trail in the Rockies. The flower-filled meadows feature a number of tiny lakes, that Samuel Allen named Minnestimma Lakes – the "sleeping waters." Many hikers have their lunch here before returning. Please, keep to beaten paths. The many visitors have caused excessive damage to vegetation in recent years.

Lyall's Larch

Lyall's larch is an uncommon coniferous tree that grows near treeline in the Rockies. Though the Larch looks similar to the Tamarack, the needles of Lyall's larch turn gold and fall off in the autumn. The Lyall's larch sheds its foliage to conserve energy through seven months of winter.

Lyall's larch frequently forms pure stands in the treeline forest south of Bow Pass. The tree grows to 10-13 m, though usually it is much shorter. Its branches are often twisted and gnarled, giving the tree a ragged appearance. Soft pale green needles grow each summer on dwarf twigs of the supple younger branches. The tree was named for David Lyall, Scottish naturalist and surgeon, of the Palliser Expedition (1857-60).

19. Bow Lake

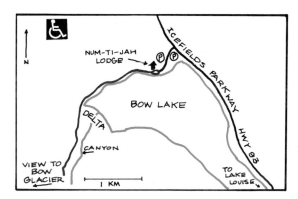

The area around Bow Lake presents a walking and a hiking option. Casual walkers may make a 400 m loop to the lakeshore and lodge, returning to the parking lot along the road. Those wishing a longer outing may continue west along the lakeshore from the lodge, eventually reaching an unmarked viewpoint overlooking the forefield of Bow Glacier. Both outings feature splendid views of Bow Lake and Bow Glacier.

With an area of 364 hectares (900 acres), Bow Lake is the third largest lake in Banff National Park.

Trailhead: Icefields Parkway (Highway 93), 37 km north of Lake Louise. Follow the Num-ti-Jah Lodge access road for 400 m, and park in the public parking lot. The trailhead is across from the public rest room.

Ratings: Num-ti-Jah loop, easy, 400 m; Bow Glacier trail, harder, 3.4 km

Lighting: morning

It is also the headwaters of the Bow River. The lake is fed by meltwater from Bow Glacier, one of six outlet valley glaciers of the 40 sq km Wapta Icefield.

Pioneer guide and outfitter, Jimmy Simpson, spent the winters of the early 1900s hunting and trapping in the remote country north of Bow Lake, and found the area much to his liking. In 1922, he began to build a simple log cabin on the lakeshore, the forerunner of today's Num-ti-Jah (numm-TAH-zjaah) Lodge. The lodge's name is a Stoney word for the American marten, a member of the weasel family that inhabits the surrounding subalpine forest.

The lodge became popular with mountaineers. With construction of the Icefields Parkway in the 1930s, Simpson expanded the lodge to capitalize on his opportunity for commercial success.

Beyond the lodge, the Bow Glacier trail skirts the lakeshore for 1.5 km to the delta at the main inlet. Climbing gradually away from this gravelly area, you reach the edge of a canyon. This canyon is noted for its "natural bridge" – a massive boulder lodged across its opening.

A few hundred metres beyond, you will reach the crest of a terminal moraine. This moraine marks the greatest advance of Bow Glacier during the Little Ice Age. One hundred and fifty years ago, the entire area between here and the cliffs was covered by glacial ice. The prominent waterfall that you see on the lower cliff drains from a concealed tarn, called Iceberg Lake. Travel beyond this viewpoint is not recommended. The trail is faint and there are no bridges across the streams.

Photo opposite: Bow Lake is the third largest lake in Banff National Park. Fed by Bow Glacier, it is the main source of the Bow River.

Deltas

Since most streams and rivers in the Rockies originate in glaciers, their waters contain a high concentration of rubble and sediment. When the angle of a stream bed is relatively steep, all this sediment can be transported by the water. But when the angle lessens, large particles begin to drop out of the flow, creating a rocky fan-shaped landform. If this landform occurs on the side of a valley, it is called an alluvial fan. If it occurs on the shore of a lake, it is known as a delta.

Bow Lake features two prominent deltas, one of them across the lake from the lodge, where meltwater from Bow Glacier enters the lake. The constant build-up of gravels, and the shifting position of the meltwater streams, prevents the growth of much vegetation.

Less obvious is the delta where the lodge sits. The stream that created this delta is now a mere trickle, and no longer transports glacial sediments. It is thought that this delta was created thousands of years ago, by a meltwater surge from a glacier near Bow Pass. This glacier has since disappeared.

20. **Bow Summit**

Trailhead: Icefields
Parkway (Highway
93), 42 km north of
Lake Louise. Use the
first parking lot on the
Bow Summit access
road.
Rating: easy, 350 m,
paved. Wheelchair
accessible from the
upper parking lot,
100 m
Lighting: anytime

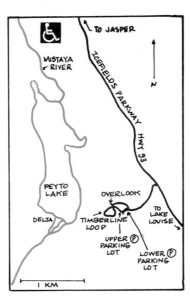

The short walk to the Peyto (PEE-toe) Lake overlook at Bow Summit takes the visitor through the treeline forest of the upper subalpine ecoregion – the land of wind flowers and wind timber – to one of the most spectacular viewpoints in the Rockies.

At an elevation of 2069 m (6787 ft), Bow Pass is the highest point in Canada crossed by a paved road that is open all year. The first thing you will notice as you step out of your vehicle, is that it is colder here than it was at Lake Louise or Banff. The high elevation of Bow

Pass would normally account for a temperature 3°C cooler than at Lake Louise. However, the chilling mass of the nearby Wapta Icefield makes Bow Summit even colder. Do not be surprised if the day has a wintry feel, even in mid-summer. Dress warmly, especially if it is windy.

Bow Summit is not a mountaintop, but a height of land that separates waters flowing south to the Bow River, from those flowing north to the Mistaya (miss-TAY-ah) River. In describing this watershed divide, the words "summit" and "pass" are used interchangeably. Located on a shoulder of Mt. Jimmy Simpson, the slopes of Bow Summit are buffetted by glacially cooled winds that deliver 6 m of annual snowfall, and cause repeated freezing and thawing.

The Treeline Forest

The forest at Bow Summit is coniferous: Engelmann spruce, subalpine fir, and whitebark pine. On the lower slopes near the parking lot, the trees are widely scattered and of normal height. But on the upper slopes, stunted tree islands are all that can grow. Why? These upper slopes are more than twice as windy as those a hundred metres lower. Wind dries out vegetation, making growth difficult and slow. The gnarled and twisted trees that result are known by the German expression krummholz, which means "crooked wood."

Subalpine fir is recognized by its silvery bark. It is more tolerant of harsh conditions than Engelmann spruce. Thus, firs are usually more numerous in the krummholz. They are able to take root either from seeds, or by sending down shoots from their branches. These trees spend much of the year covered in snow, and develop snow mould – a black growth that covers the lower branches.

The upright Engelmann spruce have a more scaly, reddish-brown bark, and they grow from seeds that develop in the sheltered centres of the mats of fir. The spruce frequently display branches only on their eastern

Krummholz

The upper slopes of Bow Summit feature stunted tree islands of Engelmann spruce and subalpine fir known as krummholz ("crooked wood" in German). In winter, exposed tree branches freeze and die. Krummholz firs survive by growing more horizontally than vertically. In this manner, they remain insulated within the snowpack, protected from the wind for much of the year. The photo shows several spruce trees growing from within a mat of fir.

Photo opposite: Peyto Lake, fifth largest lake in Banff National Park, as seen from the overlook at Bow Summit. The lake was named for Bill Peyto, pioneer outfitter and trail guide.

sides. They are said to "flag" the wind.

Despite waxy needles and thick sap, the new krummholz growth of each summer cannot withstand the cold winds of the following winter. Only branches that are insulated within the snowpack are spared this natural pruning. The krummholz firs have adapted to harsh reality by growing horizontally so that their branches will remain protected within the snow. Dense, twisted mats of fir result.

Snowdrifts accumulate in the lee of the krummholz stands. These drifts often take all summer to melt, and provide a constant water supply for wildflowers, in an area where only one-quarter of the precipitation falls as rain.

The Subalpine Meadows

Flower-filled glades of subalpine meadow are interspersed within the treeline forest. One of the first flowers to bloom is the glacier lily. Its nodding yellow flower will often poke through receding snowbanks. The bulb of the glacier lily is a favourite food of bears. Other common wildflowers in these meadows are: valerian, yellow columbine, Indian paintbrush, bracted lousewort, fleabane, arnica, black-tipped groundsel, white globe flower, mountain heather, and everlasting. Varieties of anemone (an-EMM-owe-nee), including western anemone and Drummond's anemone, also grow here. Anemone means "wind flower" and these members of the buttercup family thrive in this windy location.

Glacier lily, anemone, and other upper subalpine wildflowers manage their rapid bursts of early summer growth because their bulbs and root systems store energy gathered from sunshine the previous summer. At Bow Summit, these perennial flowers have only six weeks to flower and seed. The stored energy allows them to do this even at temperatures below freezing. Without such adaptation, a few shorter-than-average summers would kill them off. The flowers are usually at their peak in the third week of July.

Peyto Lake Overlook

From the overlook there is the most spectacular trailside view of a glacial lake in the Rockies. Three hundred metres (1000 ft) below, Peyto Lake, fifth largest in Banff National Park, stretches before you. The lake is three kilometres long and 1 kilometre wide, and is fed by meltwater from Peyto Glacier.

On the opposite side of the lake is Caldron Peak, and to the south (left), the turreted form of Peyto Peak. The toe of Peyto Glacier is concealed from view in a canyon to the viewer's left. The glacier has receded two kilometres in the last century. The massive delta at the lake's inlet has been built from glacial debris deposited by the meltwater stream. The outlet is dammed by mounds of forested moraine.

Peyto Lake is named for "Wild" Bill Peyto, noted trail guide and park warden. An immigrant from England, Peyto arrived in the Rockies in the early 1890s. He readily adapted to the backwoods life – hunting, trapping, and staking mineral claims. He began work as a trail guide in 1893. He guided several important mountaineering expeditions, including the one which discovered the Columbia Icefield in 1898. During expeditions that camped at Bow Lake, Peyto would sometimes steal away after chores to this viewpoint for some peace and quiet. Thus, the beautiful waters below the viewpoint became known as "Peyto's Lake."

The viewpoint area is populated by least chipmunk, golden-mantled ground squirrel, and a few pika. The meadows at Bow Summit are inhabited by Columbian ground squirrels, and the chatter of red squirrels from the treetops greets the visitor.

For those who wish to spend more time in the upper subalpine, the Timberline Trail is recommended. As you leave the overlook, you have a choice of three paths. The left-hand path returns to the lower parking lot; the centre path to the upper parking lot; and the right-hand path leads to the 600 m Timberline loop. Interpretive panels on this trail explain more about the harsh life of vegetation in the upper subalpine ecoregion.

Colour of Glacial Lakes

What is the most frequently asked question in the Canadian Rockies? ...*Why is the lake that colour?*...The answer: Glaciers created the lakes, and glaciers give them their colours.

Glaciers grind up bedrock, creating rock rubble and sediments of all sizes. The sediments are transported by glacier ice and meltwater. When the meltwater enters a lake, the stream velocity decreases. The larger sediments drop out of the flow, building a delta, and the smaller sediments disperse into the water. Eventually, most of these sediments settle to the lake bottom, leaving only the tiniest particles suspended in the water. These tiny clay-sized particles, called rock flour, distribute themselves evenly throughout the lake.

The tiny size of the rock-flour particles enable them to reflect the blue and green parts of the light spectrum. Thus, glacial lakes take on the rich and remarkable hues renowned worldwide. Lake colours become more pronounced as the glacier melt season progresses and the density of rock flour in the water increases. Viewing from above enhances the effect.

At Peyto Lake, muddy sediment plumes are often visible just beyond the delta. These plumes indicate where the meltwater stream disperses its sediment load into the lake (see photo).

21. **Mistaya Canyon**

Photo above: Mistaya Canyon has been eroded into a limestone step at the mouth of the Mistaya Valley.

Trailhead: Icefields Parkway (Highway 93), 72 km north of Lake Louise; 5.5 km south of the junction with Highway 11
Rating: moderate, 450 m
Lighting: afternoon

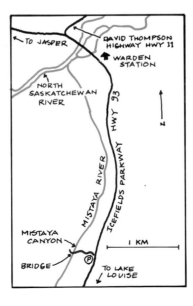

The trail to Mistaya (miss-TAY-yah) Canyon leads down along an old road-bed, to a bridge over the Mistaya River. It is an excellent place for families to take a break from driving the Icefields Parkway.

During the last ice age, the North Saskatchewan valley was eroded more deeply than the Mistaya Valley. When the ice age ended, the Mistaya River plunged over a high waterfall into the North Saskatchewan River. Since that time the silt-laden Mistaya River has eroded a deep, narrow canyon into the limestone step at the mouth of the Mistaya Valley. The Mistaya River descends 120 metres in a distance of just three kilometres.

A sturdy bridge spans the brink of the canyon. From it, you can see an unusual feature. Downstream, the canyon opening makes a series of short, symmetrical dogleg turns. The river has followed a joint set, a system of parallel cracks in the bedrock. Potholes and a natural arch are other erosional features that can be seen.

Upstream from the canyon, Mt. Sarbach is prominent. This 3155 m (10,352 ft) peak was named for Peter Sarbach, the first Swiss guide to climb in Canada. He led the first ascent of Mt. Sarbach in 1897.

You normally expect to find a damp forest in the vicinity of a canyon. However, the wall of mountains that borders the western edge of the Mistaya Valley creates a rain shadow. Hence the trailside forest is dry and is dominated by lodgepole pine, with an undergrowth of buffaloberry and juniper.

Mistaya is a native word meaning "grizzly bear." Explorers originally knew the tributaries of the North Saskatchewan River by logical but confusing names. The Mistaya was the Little Fork; the Howse was the Middle Fork; and the stream issuing from the Saskatchewan Glacier was the North Fork. Adding confusion, the Alexandra River was known as the West Branch of the North Fork!

After a few years, the Little Fork became known as Bear River. Explorer Mary Schäffer renamed it Mistaya in 1907, in order to avoid confusion with the many other Bear creeks and Bear rivers in the Rockies.

Black Bear

Although Mistaya means "grizzly bear," the black bear is more likely to be seen in the vicinity of Mistaya Canyon. In the open, dry forest here the black bear finds an abundance of shrubs, berries, and flowers, its favourite foods in a diet that is 75 percent vegetarian. The red and amber fruits of buffaloberry are one of the most important foods.

The adult male black bear is slightly less than a metre tall at the shoulder, and weighs approximately 170 kg. The coat is not always black. Cinnamon-coloured bears are fairly common. When the coat is black, there is often a small white patch on the chest.

As with grizzlies, female black bears mate every other year. The litter is normally two or three cubs, born in the den during winter dormancy. The black bear is an adept tree climber and will use this tactic to escape its two enemies – man and grizzly bears. Recent study has reversed a long-standing misconception about the bear population in the Rockies. It is now thought that there are fewer black bears than grizzly bears. A population of only 50 to 60 black bears is estimated for Banff National Park.

22. **Parker Ridge**

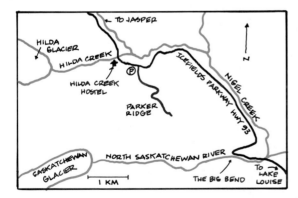

Trailhead: Icefields Parkway (Highway 93), 118 km north of Lake Louise; 9 km south of the Icefield Centre

Rating: harder, 2.4 km

Lighting: morning

The Parker Ridge trail climbs steeply through a transition zone between upper subalpine forest and alpine tundra to provide quick access to a ridgetop environment. From the ridge, the hiker obtains a panoramic view of the Saskatchewan Glacier and the southeastern fringe of the Columbia Icefield. The ridge is often cold and windy. Carry warm clothing, including gloves and a hat.

The Parker Ridge trailhead is located in a treeline forest. High elevation, cold glacial air, nearly constant winds, poor soils, avalanches, and a northeast-facing slope combine to hinder the growth of vegetation. Leaving the parking lot, the trail crosses a subalpine meadow. This meadow is a frost hollow, typical of areas near glaciers. Cold air from Hilda Glacier collects here, creating a local growing season so short that mature trees cannot develop.

Across the meadow, the climb begins. The trail enters a small but ancient forest. At one point you must squeeze between two massive Engelmann spruce trees, which are probably at least 400 years old. But most of the vegetation here is in stunted krummholz form. The gnarled, dense evergreen mats with silvery bark are subalpine firs. Although they appear to be shrubs, these are mature trees, many decades old.

On your way to the ridgetop you will see dozens of signs indicating where shortcut trails have been closed. By the late 1970s, heavy traffic and uneducated hiking practice combined to transform the slopes of Parker Ridge into a maze of trails. Vegetation was trampled and erosion was widespread. The trail was rehabilitated in a costly project. Seeds from plants on Parker ridge were grown in greenhouses, and the resulting plants were transplanted back to the ridge. Please help protect the area and this investment by keeping to the gravel path.

The treeless areas on the northeast slope of Parker Ridge are avalanche-swept rock or tundra. The tundra is composed of sedges, white mountain avens, mountain heather, snow willow, arctic willow, and everlasting. In some areas, the thin rocky soil supports only rock lichen colonies and a few alpine grasses. Vegetation grows close to the ground

Photo opposite: The view from Parker Ridge features the 9 km-long Saskatchewan Glacier, Castleguard Mountain, and the southeastern edge of Columbia Icefield.

Horn Mountain

The summits of the higher mountains in the Rockies protruded above the kilometre-thick ice sheets during the Wisconsin Glaciation. Since the retreat of the ice sheet, alpine glaciation has continued on the upper reaches of the mountains, frequently creating a mountain shape known as a horn mountain or horn.

When cirque and niche glaciers form on adjacent mountain sides, they erode downwards into the rock, creating depressions separated from each other by sharp-crested ridges called arêtes (a-RETTS). If three or more sides of the mountain are eroded in this fashion, the pyramid-like, horn shape will result.

The most famous horn mountain in the world is the Matterhorn on the border of Switzerland and Italy. There are many well-known horn mountains, including Mt. Everest. When viewed from the Parker Ridge trailhead, Mt. Athabasca and its outlier, Hilda Peak, are fine examples.

to reduce wind exposure. And thick, waxy leaves help retain moisture.

More than 6 m of snow falls at Parker Ridge each year. Because of the shaded northeast slope and cold temperatures (due to elevation and nearness to Columbia Icefield), this snow lasts well into summer. The slopes of Parker Ridge are popular with skiers in winter and spring, but don't be surprised if you see some diehards carving turns on a Parker Ridge snowpatch in midsummer.

After a steady climb, the trail gains the open ridge at an elevation of 2260 m (7450 ft). From here, follow the beaten path to the left for 500 m to a viewpoint overlooking the Saskatchewan Glacier.

Saskatchewan Glacier

The Saskatchewan Glacier is nine kilometres long and is an outlet valley glacier of Columbia Icefield. One of the longest glaciers in the Rockies, the Saskatchewan Glacier drops 750 m from the icefield rim to terminate in a marginal lake, the headwaters of the North Saskatchewan River. Unlike Athabasca Glacier, Saskatchewan Glacier has no icefalls and very few large crevasses. Of interest is a medial moraine, a strip of dark rock rubble running lengthwise on the glacier's surface. This moraine forms where two tributary glaciers merge. Saskatchewan is Cree for "swift current." Mt. Saskatchewan is the high craggy peak protruding above the rounded

summits, 8 km south of Parker Ridge.

Castleguard Cave

Immediately south (left) of the head of the Saskatchewan Glacier is Castleguard Mountain. South of this mountain is the entrance to Castleguard Cave, one of the largest cave systems in Canada. Eighteen kilometres of passages have been discovered and explored. Some of these follow an ancient glacial drainage beneath Columbia Icefield. If the day is clear, the view beyond Castleguard Mountain will include the icy summit of Mt. Bryce, 3487m (11,507ft), 19 km distant.

The Ridge Crest

If you look uphill along the crest of Parker Ridge, you will notice the outlying ridge is rounded in appearance, becoming much more rugged towards Mt. Athabasca (west). The rounded parts of the ridge were completely covered by the ice of the Wisconsin Glaciation, and the jagged areas were not. If you choose to explore along the ridge to the cairn at the high point, 2350 m (7710 ft), please stay on the beaten path. The ridge crest features krummholz forms of whitebark pine, a common tree in windy locations and fossil corals called *Syringopora*. Please do not remove the fossils.

Mountain goat, white-tailed ptarmigan, gray jay, Clark's nutcracker, pika, and raven are commonly observed on Parker Ridge. Grizzly bear, wolverine, and golden eagle may also be seen.

Mountain Goat

Parker Ridge is home range for a herd of mountain goats. These animals are easily distinguished from bighorn sheep. The goat has a white or cream-coloured coat, and black horns that are never shed. The bighorn sheep has a light brown coat with a tawny rump patch and brown horns. Mountain goats live in small herds high on mountainsides, occasionally venturing to mineral licks in the valley bottoms. Grassy ledges and slopes that offer quick escape to nearby cliffs are their favourite habitat. Grasses make up three-quarters of their diet. Not a true goat, the mountain goat is more closely related to mountain antelopes of Asia.

To a casual observer, the horns of both sexes of mountain goat appear identical. The best indicator that a mountain goat is female is if a kid is tagging along. The offspring, born in June, stay with the mother for a year.

The mountain goat is the master of alpine ridge, cliff edge, and mountaintop. Nature has equipped the mountain goat with remarkable hooves, tendons, and muscles that allow it to range over the steepest terrain with ease. The split hoof is a soft pad surrounded by a hard, bony shell. The soft pad grips like a suction cup on steep slabs, and the bony exterior can be used to lever upwards on tiny ledges. The strong muscles and tendons allow the mountain goat to leap from ledge to ledge, and cushion the shock upon landing. The mountain goat is able to turn around on narrow ledges by standing on its front legs, and walking its rear legs around on the cliff above.

Despite the fact that goats are so well-adapted and spend much of their time in hazardous areas, they seem nonchalant about certain dangers. The author has seen a goat bedded down on a snow cornice – overhanging a thousand metre cliff. Avalanches, rockfall, and starvation account for most of the natural mortality. Cougar and golden eagles are the main predators; occasionally they achieve success by attacking from above. It is common to see the nanny standing over her kid to protect it from this threat.

It is estimated that there are 800 to 900 mountain goats in Banff National Park. There are thought to be about 400 mountain goats in Yoho National Park, and 200 in Kootenay National Park. Kootenay and Mt. Robson parks use the mountain goat as their emblems.

OTHER WALKS AND HIKES IN BANFF NATIONAL PARK

Banff and the Bow Valley

See map on page 11

23. Johnson Lake

Trailhead: Follow Banff Avenue 3 km east from town to Highway 1. Keep straight ahead on the Lake Minnewanka Road. Turn east (right) at 1.2 km for Two Jack and Johnson lakes. After 3.3 km turn south (right). Follow this road 2.3 km to Johnson Lake.
Rating: easy, 2.4 km loop
Lighting: anytime

Johnson Lake is an artificial reservoir, and a popular swimming hole with Banff locals. The pleasant loop trail around its shore features fine views of Cascade Mountain and Mt. Rundle, as well as the opportunity to see elk and deer.

24. Stoney Squaw

Trailhead: Follow Gopher Street north out of Banff. Cross Highway 1 and follow the Mt. Norquay Road to the first parking lot at the ski area, 6 km from Banff.
Rating: harder, 2.1 km
Lighting: anytime

The Stoney Squaw trail climbs onto the 1868 m (6182 ft), forested summit of Stoney Squaw, and provides a grand view of the Bow Valley in the vicinity of the Banff townsite. The mountain was named for the heroine of a native legend. The legend tells of an injured man who lay at the mountain's base while his wife tended to him and hunted on the slopes above.

25. Vista Trail

Trailhead: Sulphur Mountain gondola, 3.5 km south of town on Mountain Avenue. Board the gondola (fee). The trail begins at the upper terminal.
Rating: easy, 500 m
Lighting: anytime

The Vista Trail provides a panorama of the Bow and Spray valleys, and the Banff townsite. The trail heads north along the crest of Sulphur Mountain to the site of an old observatory at 2281 m (7482 ft). Norman Sanson, curator of the Banff Park Museum from 1896-1942, was a regular visitor to the observatory. He made more than 1000 trips to this ridge top to gather weather information, all before the gondola was built. The north peak of Sulphur Mountain is now named for him.

26. Discovery Trail

Trailhead: Follow Cave Avenue 1 km west of the Bow River Bridge to the Cave and Basin Centennial Centre. The trail begins at the staircase to the left of the building.
Rating: Easy, 400 m loop
Lighting: anytime

The self-guiding Discovery Trail tells the story of the discovery and development of the Cave and Basin hot springs. The trail visits the upper entrance of the Cave springs and crumbly outcrops of tufa – rock deposited by the spring water. Complete this walk with a visit to the Cave pool and additional displays, all accessible from within the Cave and Basin Centre.

27. **Sundance Canyon**

Trailhead: Follow Cave Avenue 1 km west of the Bow River Bridge to the Cave and Basin Centennial Centre.
Rating: harder, 5.1 km. First 3.8 km wheelchair accessible
Lighting: morning

Sundance Canyon is located 3.8 km along a paved bike path from the Cave and Basin Centre. On the way to the canyon there are fine views along the Bow River, particularly of the dogtooth form of Mt. Louis. Sundance Canyon has been eroded into a bedrock fault at the mouth of a hanging valley. The 2.5 km canyon loop trail is best hiked clockwise. Two viewpoints overlooking the Bow Valley are featured in the descent.

28. **Silverton Falls**

Trailhead: Follow the Bow Valley Parkway (Highway 1A) to the Rockbound Lake trailhead, 29.5 km west of Banff, 200 m east of Castle Junction.
Rating: moderate, 900 m
Lighting late afternoon

Silverton Falls is one of the most picturesque waterfalls at trailside in the Rocky Mountain national parks. Follow the Rockbound Lake trail for 350 m. Take the right-hand trail branch, and follow this to Silverton Creek. Do not cross the creek! Instead, face downstream from the bridge and take the unmarked trail that ascends the slope to your right. This trail climbs to an unfenced viewpoint overlooking the uppermost of a half dozen cascades. "Silverton" refers to Silver City, the mining and railway boomtown that flourished nearby in 1884.

Lake Louise to Columbia Icefield

See map on page 37

29. **Bow River**

Trailhead: Lake Louise campground
Rating: easy/moderate/harder, loops of 2.5 to 7.2 km are possible. Wheelchair accessible
Lighting: anytime

This interpretive trail along the banks of the Bow River near Lake Louise Village is ideal for outings from the campground. There are four bridges over the Bow River, allowing loop walks of various lengths. Mt. Temple is prominent in the view south.

30. **Moraine Lakeshore**

Trailhead: From Lake Louise Village follow Lake Louise Drive 3 km to the Moraine Lake Road. Turn south (left). Follow this road 12 km to its end at Moraine Lake. The trail begins in front of the lodge.
Rating: easy, 1.5 km
Lighting: morning

This trail follows the forested shore of Moraine Lake to its inlet, providing views of the Wenkchemna Peaks.

31. **Fairview Lookout**

Trailhead: From Lake Louise Village follow Lake Louise Drive 5.5 km to the public parking lots at the lake. Paved walkways lead to the lakeshore. The Fairview Lookout/Saddleback Pass trailhead is next to the World Heritage Site monument.
Rating: moderate, 2.9 km loop
Lighting: afternoon.

Follow the Saddleback Pass trail for 200 m and turn right. The Fairview Lookout trail ascends steadily through subalpine forest to a viewpoint overlooking Lake

Louise. Interpretive panels provide information on the hotel's history. The growth of trees is gradually blocking the view of the Chateau.

It is easier to retrace your route to the Chateau than to complete the loop trail, which drops from the viewpoint to the lakeshore. This section of trail is rocky in places, and subject to flooding when the lake level is high.

32. **Warden Lake**

Trailhead: Icefields Parkway (Highway 93), 75 km north of Lake Louise; 2 km south of junction with Highway 11. Park opposite the warden station. The trailhead is on the east side of the Parkway, south of the warden station.
Rating: moderate, 2.2 km
Lighting: anytime

The hike to Warden Lake is along an old jeep road, the original highway from Red Deer into the mountains. It follows the banks of the North Saskatchewan River, which was designated a Canadian Heritage River in 1989. Warden Lake is the second and largest lake reached by this trail. The backdrop at the lake is provided by Mt. Murchison and Corona Ridge. Moose and waterfowl will often be seen here.

33. **Panther Falls**

Trailhead: Icefields Parkway, 113 km north of Lake Louise; 14 km south of the Icefield Centre. Park at the uppermost of the two viewpoints at the top of the Big Bend Hill.
Rating: moderate, 450 m
Lighting: morning

This unsigned trail departs from the south edge of the parking lot, and switchbacks down into Nigel Creek canyon. After traversing beneath a cliff, the last 50 m of trail crosses an exposed slope to an unfenced viewpoint at the base of the 60 m high falls. This is a slippery, hazardous area. Use caution.

JASPER NATIONAL PARK

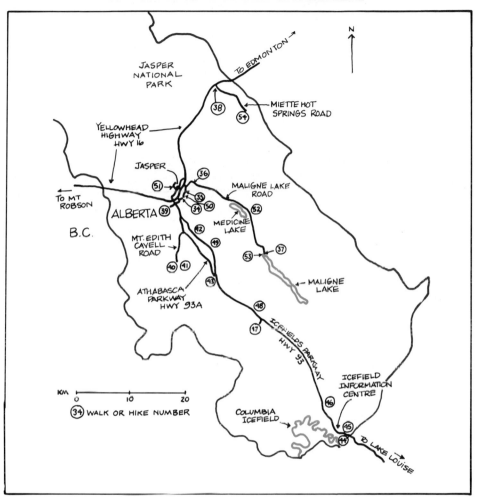

Established in 1907, Jasper National Park is the largest of the Rocky Mountain national parks. It also has the greatest variety of walking and hiking destinations. The trails described in Jasper feature: historical themes, tranquil lakes and ponds, glaciers, Columbia Icefield, alpine meadows, and a mountain summit. Many of the walks are in prime wildlife habitat. Most of the larger mammals may be seen: elk, deer, black bear, grizzly bear, bighorn sheep, mountain goats, moose, coyote, wolf and mountain caribou. Jasper is named for Jasper Hawes, manager of the North West Company's fur trade outpost in the Athabasca Valley, in 1817.

34. **Old Fort Point**

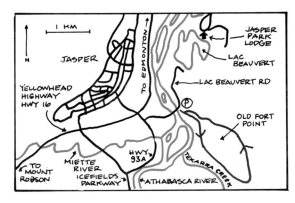

The trail to Old Fort Point climbs steeply to the crest of a rocky landform south of Jasper, providing an overview of the townsite and the Athabasca Valley.

During the winter of 1811, David Thompson, explorer and fur trader with the North West Company, made an epic crossing of Athabasca Pass, thereby establishing a fur trade route. Thompson stationed one of his men, William Henry, to build an outpost in the vicinity of present day Jasper townsite. This building became known as Henry

Trailhead: Follow Highway 93A south from the intersection of Hazel Avenue and Connaught Drive in Jasper townsite.

Cross Highway 16. Turn east (left) onto the Lac Beauvert Road and follow this for 1 km. Cross the Athabasca River and

park on the east (right) side of the road.
Rating: harder, 4.5 km loop
Lighting: anytime

House, the first permanent European habitation in the Rockies.

For decades, there has been controversy as to the exact location of Henry House. Historians have studied original accounts and diaries. Unfortunately, these accounts offer contradictory information as to the specific location of the building. In addition, it appears there may have been several buildings called "Henry House," constructed over a period of several decades.

Recently, it has been suggested that Old Fort Point may be a corruption of Old *Ford* Point. A ford is a natural shallow, or series of islands that allow relatively easy crossing of a river. If true, then Old Fort Point may not have had any connection with the location of Henry House.

It is best to hike the Old Fort Point loop in a counterclockwise direction, beginning with the staircase. In this fashion, the first kilometre of the hike is fairly steep, but the remainder involves a gradual descent. At the top of the staircase, a plaque designates the Athabasca River as a Canadian Heritage River. The Athabasca River is 1230 km long and rises at the north edge of Columbia Icefield. Its waters eventually reach the Arctic Ocean by way of the Mackenzie River system. To-

gether with its tributaries, the Athabasca River drains most of the area of Jasper National Park.

From the heritage river plaque, the trail continues its steady climb onto the arid crest of Old Fort Point, revealing a splendid 360-degree panorama of the Athabasca and Miette valleys, including Jasper townsite. Old Fort Point is sparsely vegetated with Douglas fir, juniper, and grasses. The view alone would have made it a good location for an outpost. But hauling water up the slope from the river would have been a chore!

Leaving the high point, the trail descends into a grove of trembling aspen and loops back to the parking lot through a damp pine forest. There is a maze of trails in this area. Follow signs for Trail #1 or #1A at all junctions.

Photo opposite:
Pyramid Mountain provides the backdrop for Jasper townsite in this view from Old Fort Point. This landform is located where the Miette and Athabasca valleys merge.

Roche Moutonée

Old Fort Point is a *roche moutonée* (ROSH moot-on-AY). This French expression means "fleecy rock." A roche moutonée is a resistant hillock of bedrock carved by glacier ice. In this classic example, the shape indicates the direction that the glacier flowed. The smooth, streamlined slope faced into the flow of ice, and the jagged, cliff-like side faced away. The streamlined slope of Old Fort Point faces the Athabasca River.

35. Annette Lake

Trailhead: Follow Highway 16 east from Jasper, 3.7 km to the Maligne Lake Road. Turn east (right) and cross the Athabasca River. Turn south (right) onto the Jasper Park Lodge Road and follow it for 1.4 km. Then turn east (left) and drive another 600 m to the second parking area.
Rating: easy, 2.4 km paved loop. Wheelchair accessible
Lighting: anytime

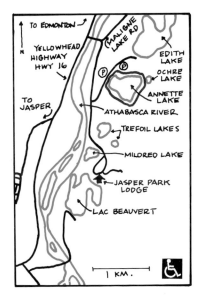

The paved trail around Annette Lake is one of the few trails in the mountain national parks designed to allow wheelchair access. The project was made possible by a grant from the Clifford E. Lee Foundation in 1981, the International Year of Disabled Persons.

There are more than 800 lakes and ponds in Jasper National Park. Many occupy glacially formed hollows in bedrock. Others are beaver ponds or backwaters of large rivers like the Athabasca. Annette Lake and the other lakes near Jasper Park Lodge are kettle ponds. They were created when large blocks of ice detached as glaciers retreated 11,000 years ago. As the ice blocks slowly melted, they created depressions in the glacial rubble. Silts then accumulated in the bottoms of the depressions, plugging cracks in the rubble, allowing the lakes to form. It is thought that Annette Lake resulted from the joining of three kettle ponds.

Where does the water in Annette Lake come from today? Not from glacial melt. Rainfall, runoff, and springs account for most of the inflow. However, studies of the Maligne Karst System, have shown that some of the water that disappears underground at Medicine Lake emerges at Annette Lake and the other lakes near Jasper Park Lodge. Annette Lake has no visible outlet.

There are many kettle ponds in the Rockies, and most will eventually fill with aquatic vegetation. Soils will collect among the growth, allowing trees to take root. Then the lake bottom will be slowly reclaimed as part of the surrounding forest.

At its northeastern end, the trail separates Annette Lake from the swampy waters of Ochre Lake. The bottom of Ochre Lake is quicksand; for your safety, please keep out. From the south shore of Annette Lake, the view north shows the division between the front ranges and the eastern main ranges. The gray, steeply tilted limestone peaks of the front ranges are to the east (right), and

the reddish, more angular, quartzite peaks of the eastern main ranges are to the west (left). The thrust fault that separates them is slightly west (left) of the massive cliff of the Palisade.

Elk will often be seen near Annette Lake, and a pair of loons usually nests on the waters. On hot summer days people from Jasper flock to the lake to take a dip. The surface water may reach 20°C – hot for the Rockies. The lake was named for Annette Rogers, wife of an early superintendent of Jasper National Park.

Photo opposite: Annette Lake is one of seven kettle ponds on the east bank of the Athabasca River near Jasper. From the shores of the lake, there are wonderful views of the mountains near the townsite. Here, Signal Mountain is seen at sunrise.

Roche Bonhomme
("Old Man Mountain") 2495 m (8186 ft)

Roche Bonhomme (ROSH bun-OMM) is a summit in the Colin Range northeast of Jasper, and is prominent in the view from the townsite. The name means "good fellow rock" in French. The arrangement of slabby rock layers near the mountain crest bears a striking resemblance to the face of a man, looking skyward. See if it reminds you of anyone you know.

It is thought that many of the French names in the Athabasca Valley were given by the voyageurs of the fur trade between 1811 and 1850. So Roche Bonhomme has been a well known landmark in the Athabasca Valley for almost two centuries.

36. **Maligne Canyon**

Maligne Canyon is the most interesting limestone canyon in the Canadian Rockies. Its maximum depth is 55 m, yet in places it is scarcely a metre wide.

Trailheads: Follow Highway 16, 3.7 km east from Jasper to the Maligne Lake Road. Turn right. On the Maligne Lake Road there are three trailheads for the canyon: Sixth Bridge (turnoff at km 2.3), Fifth Bridge (turnoff at km 3.1), and Maligne Canyon Loop (turnoff at km 6.3).
Ratings: Sixth Bridge, harder, 3.7 km; Fifth Bridge, moderate 2.7 km; and Maligne Canyon Loop, easy 0.8 km loop
Lighting: early afternoon

O ne early visitor remarked: "Any other canyon is like a crack in a tea cup".

The three trailheads at Maligne (muh-LEEN) Canyon allow the walker to choose different experiences. The short Maligne Canyon Loop from the teahouse is on a paved path, and provides quick access to the canyon's highlights. The longer uphill walks from the Fifth and Sixth bridges are on rougher trails, but allow a greater appreciation of the canyon's features.

A blueprint for the Rockies was revealed 11,000 years ago, at the end of the last ice age (the Wisconsin Glaciation). The major valleys had been more deeply eroded by the glaciers than their smaller tributaries. Thus, the floors of the tributary valleys were left hanging above the main valleys.

The Maligne is one such hanging valley. Initially, the Maligne River would have plunged into the Athabasca Valley as a waterfall. But over the course of thousands of years, the Maligne River has followed cracks in the limestone bedrock near the mouth of the valley, and eroded the 2 km-long Maligne Canyon. With a maximum depth of 55 m near Second Bridge, the canyon is one of the most spectacular in the Rockies.

How the Canyon Was Formed

Maligne Canyon is being eroded by three processes: abrasion by silt-laden glacial meltwater; dissolution of the limestone bedrock by naturally acidic rainwater; and the collapse of canyon walls by the hydraulic force of the water torrent. The highest waterfall, 23 m, is just above the First Bridge. Here, the entire volume of the river is forced through a narrow breach before plunging over the precipice.

The upper canyon has been eroded through tough limestone of the 360-million-year-old Palliser Formation. In many places, the canyon is scarcely a metre wide. The narrowness indicates that the limestone is hard, and erosion has been rapid. In geological terms, "rapid" in this case is 0.5 cm (0.2 inches) per year.

Life: Present and Past

The narrow, vertical world of the canyon is home to pack rats, mice, and ravens, whose nests are visible on the canyon walls. Maligne Canyon is one of few nesting sites in Alberta for the black swift. The American dipper (water ouzel) will also be seen here.

The airborne spray generated by the waterfalls, coats the canyon walls and edges. The spray helps plants to grow within the canyon and on the rim nearby.

The limestone rocks of Maligne Canyon contain many fossils: snail-like gastropods, clam-like brachiopods, squid-like cephalopods, crinoids (related to starfish), and corals. Two prominent examples of fossils are displayed in the upper canyon, between the teahouse and the First Bridge. Please do not touch them.

The Maligne Valley

The Maligne Valley is a strike valley. The valley and the course of the Maligne River follow a major fault in the earth's crust. The fault marks the division between the 360-million-year-old limestones of the front ranges to the east, and the 570-million-year-old quartzite of the eastern main ranges to the west. (Please note: this is not the age of the mountains, but of the bedrock that comprises them). The front range peaks of the Colin and Queen Elizabeth ranges were uplifted 85 million years ago, and feature a steeply tilted, sawtooth mountain shape.

Medicine Lake, located 17 km south of Maligne Canyon, is the only disappearing lake in the Rockies. It drains into an underground waterway, emerging in Maligne Canyon and some of the lakes near Jasper Park Lodge. Every autumn, the water level drops dramatically and the lake "disappears," leaving an expansive flat where wildlife are often seen.

The rounded quartzite summits of the Maligne Range formed 120 million years ago, and were totally enveloped in ice sheets during the Wisconsin Glaciation.

If you look carefully at some of the boulders at trailside, you will notice they are different from the rock in the canyon walls. These boulders are glacial erratics – rocks transported by the glaciers and deposited here when the ice receded. Glaciologists use the erratics to find out where the glacier ice came from.

The Maligne Karst System

Maligne Canyon is spectacular, but the Maligne Valley contains an even more remarkable, invisible feature – an underground river system. The ability of rainwater and runoff to dissolve limestone allows cracks in the bedrock to enlarge into deep fissures. When connected, these fissures become subterranean caves and waterways, known as Karst.

To fully appreciate the nature of the Maligne Karst System, we must trace the Maligne River from its headwaters in the Brazeau Icefield, 80 kilometres south of Maligne Canyon. The glacial meltwater from Brazeau Icefield initially collects in Maligne Lake, then flows on the surface to Medicine Lake, 17 km south of Maligne Canyon. However, at Medicine Lake the lake level fluctuates dramatically during the year.

Before the road was constructed along the east shore of Medicine Lake, a boat service shuttled tourists across it. But the fluctuating lake level played havoc with boat traffic. So, attempts were made to plug holes found on the lake bottom with newspapers and even mattresses.

The holes at the bottom of Medicine Lake are sinkholes. They allow the lake to drain into an underground waterway at the rate of 24,000 litres per second. During the snowmelt of spring and early summer, the sinkholes cannot drain the lake fast enough and the lake level rises. In some years Medicine Lake overflows into the normally dry riverbed at its northern end. By late summer, as the snowmelt season ends, the sink holes drain the lake faster than water flows in. So the water level drops dramatically. By autumn, all that remains of Medicine Lake is a braided stream on an expansive mud flat – a good place to observe moose, elk, and caribou.

The topography produced by an underground drainage system of this kind is called karst. The Maligne Karst System has been very well studied. The underground waterway, though 17 km long, is too narrow to allow much access for cavers, even during low water. However, dyes have been released into Medicine Lake, and by observing where they emerge, many of the karst outlets have been found. Most of the water that disappears at Medicine Lake emerges downstream from the Fourth Bridge in Maligne Canyon. Some of it also feeds lakes in the vicinity of Jasper Park Lodge.

The water you see upstream from the Fourth Bridge in Maligne Canyon has not journeyed underground, but has collected in a normal fashion on the surface. So, there are two Maligne Rivers between Medicine Lake and Maligne Canyon – one on the surface, and one underground. However, the exact nature of the underground system remains unknown.

Potholes

Potholes are circular depressions, drilled into bedrock at falls and rapids by the circling water current. At first, the water current spins sand and pebbles trapped in a slight depression. These particles act like drill bits. As the pothole develops, large boulders are used. If, after centuries, the stream changes course, the pothole may be left high and dry, often with the rounded pebbles in place. Some potholes eventually fill with silt and thin soils, and become hanging gardens on canyon walls, where ferns, mosses, shrubs, and even small trees take root.

37. **Maligne Lake**

Trailhead: Follow Highway 16, 3.7 km east from Jasper to the Maligne Lake Road. Turn east (right) on the Maligne Lake Road. Follow it 44 km to the parking lots on the east side of Maligne Lake. The trail begins in front of Maligne Lake Chalet and heads south.
Rating: moderate, 3.2 km loop
Lighting: anytime

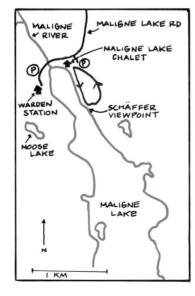

The trail to Schäffer Viewpoint on Maligne Lake follows the lake's east shore to a prominent bay, where interpretive signs describe the lake's exploration in 1908.

Maligne Lake, the largest in the Canadian Rockies, is 22 km long, has an area of 2066 hectares (5103 acres), and a maximum depth of 96 m. The average width is about 1 km. The lake is fed by meltwater from the Brazeau (brah-ZOE) Icefield, and the other glaciers on the mountains that you can see, 30 km to the south. Large lakes often owe their existence to some kind of dam – natural or otherwise. Maligne Lake is no exception. Its outlet is dammed by the largest known rockslide in the Canadian Rockies. With an estimated volume of 498 million cubic metres, this rockslide is more than 13 times the size of the Frank Slide in Crowsnest Pass.

Until 1908, Maligne Lake was one of the best kept secrets in the Rockies. Henry MacLeod, a surveyor working for the Canadian Pacific Railway, reached the lake from the north in 1875. His report was hardly the kind of advertising to drum up interest. Fed up with the difficult trail from the Athabasca Valley, MacLeod called Maligne, "Sorefoot Lake," and wrote it off for further exploration.

However, Stoney Natives had long known of Maligne Lake. To them it was *Chaba Imne* – Great Beaver Lake. Their reference to the lake eventually attracted the interest of white explorers. Sampson Beaver, a Stoney leader, had seen the lake when he was 14. Sixteen years later, at the request of explorer Mary Schäffer, he drew a crude map from memory. This map provided Schäffer and her party with enough clues to find the lake in 1908. Schäffer's party constructed a raft, christened the *Chaba*, and spent three days mapping the lake and naming many features.

In the view down Maligne Lake from Schäffer Viewpoint, Leah Peak (closest), and Samson Peak are on the east (left). Leah was

Sampson Beaver's wife. On the west (right) are the glaciated peaks of Mts. Charlton and Unwin. In the vicinity of these mountains, Maligne Lake narrows to a mere 200 m. This is Samson Narrows, the location of Spirit Island, and destination for a boat tour.

From Schäffer viewpoint, return along the lakeshore, or loop east to the parking lot through pleasant subalpine forest.

Photo opposite:
Maligne Lake is the largest lake in the Canadian Rockies, and one of the largest lakes in the world fed by glacier meltwater.

Moose

The moose is the largest animal with antlers in the world. It weighs up to 600 kg, and stands 2 m tall at the shoulder. Moose can run at speeds up to 55 km per hour and are capable swimmers. Aquatic plants are the animal's favourite summer foods. In winter, the moose moves to higher elevations, browsing on shrubs that protrude above the snowpack.

This animal is no longer numerous in the Rocky Mountain parks. Though wolves are the principal predator, road kills and a parasitic liver fluke have taken a heavy toll of moose in recent years. Seven moose were killed on Jasper National Park roads in 1990. The shores of Maligne Lake, and the numerous ponds and lakes immediately to the north, are among the few remaining good places to see moose, especially in early morning and evening.

38. **Pocahontas**

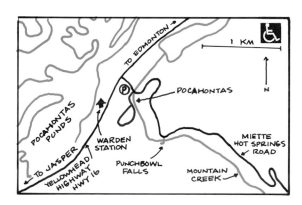

Trailhead: Follow Highway 16, east of Jasper 42.9 km to Pocahontas. Turn east (right) onto the

Miette Hot Springs Road. The trailhead is 150 m farther, on the right.

Rating: easy loop (wheelchair accessible), 1 km; harder loop, 2 km. Brochure available

Lighting: anytime

The Coal Mine Trail at Pocahontas was completed in 1991. It explores the ruins of the industrial and commercial sections of this mining town. The lower trail is paved, allowing wheelchair access to a few points of interest. The unpaved upper trail is extremely steep, particularly beneath the east viewpoint.

Pocahontas had its origin in 1908, when prospector Frank Villeneuve discovered coal on the lower slopes of Roche Miette (ROSH mee-YETT). Villeneuve was in the right place at the right time. A second transcontinental railway, the Grand Trunk Pacific, had been proposed to cross the Rockies at Jasper. The railway, using coal-fired locomotives, would pass close by the claim. Villeneuve named his mine Jasper Park Collieries. The community built nearby was named Pocahontas, after the successful coal mining town in Virginia.

Mining commenced in 1910. A commercial lower town and residential upper town developed. The upper town reportedly housed over 2000 people, making it far larger than Jasper. Most miners were immigrants from Britain, Italy, and eastern Europe.

World War I created a huge market for coal, but affairs at Pocahontas were far from happy. Bad management put the miners and their employers on poor terms. Safety problems led to a series of fatal accidents. A second railway, the Canadian Northern, was completed through Jasper in 1913. Soon, both railways were nearing economic collapse, and it was decided they should amalgamate. When this was accomplished in 1916, the superfluous railway tracks were torn up and shipped to Europe for use in the war effort. Unfortunately for Pocahontas, the tracks on south side of the Athabasca River were removed, leaving the mine without a way to export its product. Labour unrest continued. The demise of Pocahontas was assured by the general miners' strike of 1919. Thereafter, industry looked elsewhere for coal, and the mine closed permanently in April 1921.

Photo opposite: Coal was discovered in eastern Jasper National Park in 1908. Pocahontas was a mining town that developed adjacent to one of the claims. Like many mining towns, Pocahontas was a boomtown. When the mine closed in 1921, the town folded soon after. Photo, courtesy of the Glenbow Archive (Calgary)

Punchbowl Falls

An inescapable aspect of life at Pocahontas was the steep hill separating the upper and lower townsites. As they went about their business, residents were continually walking up and down the hill, and crossing Mountain Creek. This crossing was usually made at an ornate bridge above Punchbowl Falls.

Most of the rocks in the vicinity of Punchbowl Falls are relatively soft, and easily eroded. However, here Mountain

Creek has uncovered a resistant conglomerate rock, the 98 million year old Cadomin Formation. Conglomerate is a sedimentary rock containing pebbles and fragments eroded from other rock types. It looks very much like concrete. Unable to erode deeply into this rock, the creek cascades over it. The pounding of the water has eroded several plunge pools: bowl-like depressions that gave the falls their name. A 3500-year-old native archeological site has been discovered near the falls.

39. **The Whistlers**

Trailhead: Follow the Icefields Parkway 2.5 km south from Jasper to Whistlers Road. Turn west (right). Follow the Whistlers Road 4 km to the Jasper Tramway. The trailhead is at the upper terminal of the tramway (fee).
Rating: harder, 1.4 km
Lighting: anytime

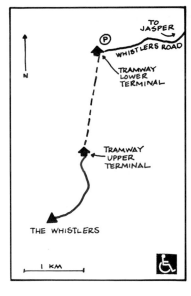

In its seven minute ride, the Jasper Tramway climbs 937 metres, whisking the visitor from forested valley bottom to the stark mountaintop environment of The Whistlers. From the upper terminal, the well-shod and warmly clothed hiker is encouraged to walk the rocky summit trail. This is the easiest way to a mountaintop in the Rockies, and at 2464 m (8084 ft), is the highest point on any trail in this book. The panorama from The Whistlers includes the Miette and Athabasca valleys, Jasper townsite, many lakes, and on clear days, Mt. Robson, the highest peak in the Canadian Rockies, 78 kilometres away.

Well above treeline, the summit of The Whistlers is the domain of strong winds, harsh sunlight, poor soils, and brief summers. Your first impression may be of a barren mountaintop. However, the rocky soils of The Whistlers support a surprising variety of alpine vegetation. The harsh conditions have dictated ingenious adaptations. Alpine plants are tiny, and hug the ground to reduce exposure to the wind. Plant leaves are often thick and waxy, to retain moisture. The colourful flowers do not live long, since energy must be conserved. Some plants are mat-like and grow outwards in a circular fashion. Frequently, the centres of the mat will die off, as the plant prunes itself and directs its energy towards new growth. The mats, both dead and growing, help prevent soil from blowing away, and also provide the opportunity for other vegetation to take root.

The Whistlers mountaintop shows characteristics of a glaciated landscape. The domed summit was completely covered by ice during the Wisconsin Glaciation. Huge blocks, known as glacial erratics, were left on the mountaintop as the glaciers receded. Several bowl-shaped depressions called cirques, were eroded into the mountainside by glaciers.

Today, repeated freezing and thawing of water trapped in rocky crevices, continues to wedge boulders apart, helping to slowly create new soil. The soil is stabilized by vegetation. Eventually, after centuries, small alpine meadows will appear.

Unfortunately, the construction of the Jasper Tramway in 1963 introduced a destructive agent of erosion to The Whistlers – the feet of human visitors. More than 150,000 people now visit the upper terminal each year. Snow patches frequently linger until midsummer, making it difficult to find and stay on the trail. A single footstep off the trail can destroy an alpine plant, obliterating decades of growth in an instant. Please make every effort to stay on the trail.

Photo opposite: The stark summit of The Whistlers is typical of mountaintop environments in the alpine ecoregion.

Hoary Marmot

The Whistlers is named for the piercing whistle of the hoary marmot. Similar to the woodchuck, this large rodent lives in the quartzite boulder fields on the mountaintop. Grasses, leaves, flowers, and berries make up its diet. Grizzly bear, lynx, and the eagle are its predators. The marmot has the perfect answer to tough times in the alpine ecoregion. When the snow flies and the going gets tough, the marmot goes to sleep. Remarkably, it hibernates nine months of the year.

40. **Path of the Glacier**

Trailhead: Follow the Icefields Parkway (Hwy 93) 7 km south from Jasper to Hwy 93A. Turn right, follow Hwy 93A south for 5.2 km. Turn right and take the Mt. Edith Cavell Road south 14.5 km to the parking lot. Trailers and large RVs cannot navigate the sharp turns of the road. Leave them at the trailer drop off on Highway 93A.
Rating: easy, 1.6 km loop
Lighting: morning

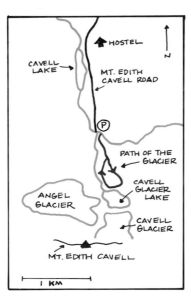

The Path of the Glacier explores the forefield of Cavell Glacier, an area that was covered by glacial ice only a century ago. This rocky trail provides spectacular views of Mt. Edith Cavell, Cavell Glacier Lake, and Cavell and Angel glaciers.

The late 1800s saw the end of a period of global glacial advance, known today as the Little Ice Age. During this advance, the ice of the two main glaciers on Mt. Edith Cavell combined to flow northwards as far as the present day parking lot. Since the 1880s, the earth's climate has been warming and these glaciers have retreated dramatically.

The initial climb from the parking lot is over a terminal moraine, a horseshoe-shaped pile of boulders and gravel pushed up by Cavell Glacier. From the crest of the moraine a view of apparent desolation unfolds. In its advance, the glacier obliterated the vegetation and centuries-old soils of a mature spruce/fir forest. In retreat, the glacier left behind a landscape of rubble.

The glacial forefield is a harsh home for vegetation. If you look closely, you will see communities of willows, sedges, and wildflowers, especially along the banks of meltwater streams. Despite this growth, less than 1 percent of the forefield is currently vegetated. It will be centuries before a mature forest becomes re-established, provided another glacial advance does not interfere.

For the next 500 m, the trail climbs gradually along the flank of a lateral moraine. After you pass the junction with the Cavell Meadows Trail, the Path of the Glacier Trail drops towards Cavell Glacier and its iceberg-dotted lake. Here, in the nearly perpetual shade of Mt. Edith Cavell, you are face-to-face with an ice-age landscape. Cavell Glacier is a cirque glacier, fed by snow and ice avalanches from the north face of Mt. Edith Cavell.

In contrast to the daunting appearance of Cavell Glacier, the winged shape of the sunlit Angel Glacier appears as a delight. The descending tongue of this glacier was separated from the Cavell Glacier in the early 1940s. Since then, the Angel Glacier has retreated slowly. The glacier presently appears to be in equilibrium, receiving enough annual snowfall to maintain its precarious position on the mountainside.

Photo opposite: The winged shape of Angel Glacier adorns the cliffs of Mt. Edith Cavell, above the Path of the Glacier Trail.

Caution:
The Mt. Edith Cavell Road receives no winter maintenance. In early and late summer, inquire at the park information centre in Jasper about road and trail conditions for the Path of the Glacier and Cavell Meadows trails.

Mt. Edith Cavell
3363 m (11,033 ft)

Natives called Mt. Edith Cavell "White Ghost," probably in reference to the snow-covered mountain's appearance in moonlight. Mt. Edith Cavell was known to the voyageurs of the fur trade in the early 1800s as "La Montagne de la Grande Traverse" (The Mountain of the Great Crossing).

When the Grand Trunk Pacific Railway reached the vicinity of Jasper in 1911, the mountain became known as Mt. Fitzhugh, after the railway's vice-president. In 1915, the name was changed to commemorate Edith Cavell, a British nurse. She was executed for assisting allied prisoners of war to escape during World War I.

41. **Cavell Meadows**

Trailhead: See Hike #40, *Path of the Glacier* for route information. Note off-season travel caution.

Rating: harder, 3.8 km

Lighting: morning

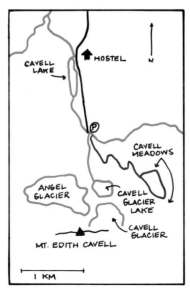

O
f the half dozen trails in this book that lead into the alpine environment, the Cavell Meadows trail docs so in perhaps the most spectacular setting.

The first 600 m of the Cavell Meadows Trail is shared with the Path of the Glacier Trail. At the junction, the Cavell Meadows Trail climbs steeply to the left over a lateral moraine – a ridge of rock debris pushed up alongside Cavell Glacier when it extended down the valley. The coarse sand underfoot has been eroded from the surrounding quartzite boulders.

Least chipmunk, golden-mantled ground squirrel, and pika live here.

At the top of the moraine, there is an abrupt transition from boulder field to forest. This is the trimline of Cavell Glacier, where ice met trees. Some trees near the trimline show evidence of roots and trunks damaged during the most recent glacial advance.

After paralleling the moraine crest for a few hundred metres, the trail resumes its climb towards the meadows above. The forest here is an ancient one, dominated by Engelmann spruce and subalpine fir. In the winter of 1990-91, a snow avalanche from the north face of Mt. Edith Cavell created a wind blast strong enough to topple some of these trees. At trailside, one spruce tree cleared by chainsaw from the avalanche debris shows 232 concentric rings. Each of these rings represents the growth of one year, giving an indication of the tree's age. See if you can find a fallen tree that was older.

Two and a half kilometres from the trailhead, the forest becomes a patchwork of tree islands, separated by glades of subalpine meadow. Although the elevation here (1860 m or 6100 ft) is low for treeline, the glacial chill prevents the growth of dense forest above this point. Soon the trail emerges from the forest completely – revealing astounding views of Angel Glacier. Keep right at the junctions, and follow the trail through a carpet of wildflowers to a knoll

with a cairn on it. From here, the trail loops back through the upper meadows to rejoin the approach trail at treeline.

The upper meadows are in the alpine ecoregion and are occasionally visited by mountain caribou and grizzly bear. Some hollows here may hold snow all year. The reddish tinge is "watermelon snow," a one-celled algae. Some of the steep slopes above the meadows contain peculiar features called rock glaciers: accumulations of rock that contain just enough ice to allow the whole mass to creep downhill.

Photo opposite: Wildflowers and spectacular views of Angel Glacier and the 1600 m (mile-high) north face of Mt. Edith Cavell are the highlights of the Cavell Meadows Trail.

Mountain Heather

Botanists call areas like the Cavell Meadows a heath tundra. "Heath" is mountain heather, one of the most common plants in the upper subalpine and alpine ecoregions. Heather frequently forms dense mats, and grows in association with everlasting, mountain avens, crowberry, grouseberry, alpine willow, and snow willow. There are four varieties of heather – two white, one pink, and one yellow. All have bell-shaped, nodding flowers. Mountain heather is an evergreen member of the family of plants that includes blueberries. However, heather is berry-less

42. **Valley of the Five Lakes**

Photo above: The five lakes in the Valley of the Five Lakes are noted for their aquamarine and jade hues.

Trailhead: Icefields Parkway (Highway 93), 11 km south of Jasper; 92 km north of the Icefield Centre
Rating: moderate, 4.6 km loop
Lighting: anytime

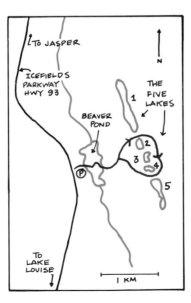

Although not glacially fed, the lakes in the Valley of the Five Lakes possess striking aquamarine and jade hues. The trail to the lakes leads through the rolling ridge country of the Athabasca Valley and offers the opportunity to see wildlife: deer, elk, beaver, waterfowl, coyote, and black bear. The vegetation is typical of the Athabasca Valley. The forest is open lodgepole pine, with undergrowth of bearberry, buffaloberry, twinflower, and juniper.

The trail initially crosses a gritstone ridge. From the ridge, the trail drops abruptly to an un-named creek that has been dammed by beavers. A boardwalk crosses the pond. Look for the beaver lodges, the dome-shaped mounds of sticks and mud. Sedges and a thicket of moisture-loving shrubs grow at the pond's edge. While doing field work the author saw a great blue heron here.

Keep straight ahead as you climb uphill from the pond. This open, sunny slope is another gritstone ridge, and supports a stand of mature, stately Douglas firs. Looking back you will see Mt. Edith Cavell, prominent in the distance. On top of the ridge, you enter a grove of trembling aspen. The trail soon forks. Take the north (left) branch, and descend from the ridge into a damper lodgepole pine forest.

The Five Lakes owe their exist-ence to the underlying bedrock of the Athabasca Valley. Parallel, up-turned ridges of resistant grit-stone are separated by weaker shales, which have been eroded into hollows. The hollows have become home to the Five Lakes, which are separated by natural dams of resistant rock.

There is a maze of trails in the vicinity of the Five Lakes. Use the accompanying map to ensure that you do not become side-tracked. The loop trail leads be-tween lakes one and two, then turns south (right) onto an open sideslope along the east shore of the second lake. The third and fourth lakes are joined by a nar-rows. It is in the fourth lake that the shades of blue and green are most pleasing.

At the end of the fourth lake, turn right across one of the rock dams to begin the return section of the loop. On the dam, a side trail to the south (left) gives a view of the fifth lake, where you may see the Common loon.

Miette Gritstone

The bedrock ridges in this part of the Athabasca Valley are composed of gritstone of the Miette (mee-YETT) Formation. Gritstone is a coarse, resistant sandstone. The Miette sediments were deposited between 730 and 570 million years ago, making the formation the oldest visible in this part of the Rockies.

The Miette sediments accumulated to a maximum thickness of 9000 m. When water seeps into cracks in rock this far underground, it becomes pressurized. Its temperature greatly exceeds the boiling point, and the water is able to dissolve minerals from the surrounding rock and transport them. The white veins you see in the Miette gritstone near the Valley of the Five Lakes, are cracks which were filled with liquefied quartz. The rock cooled when thrust to the surface during mountain building, and the quartz solution hardened into the mineral quartz.

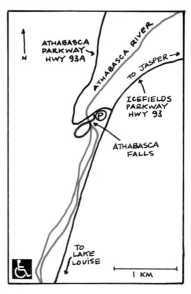

43. **Athabasca Falls**

Photo above: At Athabasca Falls, the Athabasca River thunders over a resistant formation of quartzite in the bedrock.

Trailhead: From the Icefields Parkway (Highway 93), 32 km south of Jasper, 71 km north of the Icefield Centre, turn west onto Highway 93A. follow it 500 m, and then turn left into the parking lot.

Rating: Viewpoint; wheelchair accessible

Lighting: afternoon

thabasca Falls is a "must see" for any visitor to the Rockies. A glacial river thunders over a 30 m drop just a few metres from where you stand.

In several places the trail follows watercourses abandoned when the river found a path of less resistance. The most spectacular viewpoints at the falls are on the far side of the river. Some year, the brink of the waterfall and the viewpoints it supports, will be undercut. The whole area will collapse into the river, and the falls will migrate slightly upstream. For now, please keep within the paved and fenced viewpoints. This protects the surrounding vegetation from trampling, and also protects you. Fatal slips into the falls and canyon have occurred.

Glaciers once filled the Athabasca Valley nearly to the brim, flowing north from Columbia Icefield and carving a massive

U-shaped trough. However, the ice was unable to completely smooth out the valley bottom. Some resistant rock formations endured as steps and ridges. Athabasca Falls marks the location of a resistant step, an outcrop of 570-million-year-old Gog quartzite.

Many of the waterfalls and canyons in the Rockies are in limestone formations that are relatively easily eroded. Limestone canyons are often deep, narrow, and long. Sometimes they feature high waterfalls. Because quartzite is tough, the rock step at Athabasca Falls has eroded slowly. So the falls are broader than most, and the canyon is relatively short. The rock downstream from Athabasca Falls features potholes.

Although the typical vegetation for this part of the Athabasca Valley is a dry forest of lodgepole pine, the spray generated by the falls creates a damp canyon forest next to the river. Boggy areas in the vicinity are home to black spruce, a relatively rare tree in the Rockies.

Synclines

The mountain east of Athabasca Falls is Mt. Kerkeslin (kurr-KEZZ-lin). If you look at the sedimentary layers in the mountain's northwest face, you will detect a shallow, downward fold. This U-shape is known to geologists as a syncline (SIN-cline).

When the rock that now makes up Mt. Kerkeslin was deep within the earth's crust, it was warm and pliable. The tremendous compressive forces of mountain building were able to warp it into folds. The U-shaped fold of a syncline was usually paired with an arch-shaped fold called an anticline. Rock at the base of a syncline was compressed and made more resistant to erosion. Rock at the crest of an anticline was stretched, weakened, and more easily eroded. Many major valleys in the Rockies, including the Bow and Athabasca, have been eroded by ice and water downward into the crest of anticlines. The mountain ranges parallel to the valleys have endured atop synclines.

The fold in Mt. Kerkeslin marks the northern end of the Castle Mountain Syncline, which begins at Castle Mountain in Banff and extends for 260 km northward. Mt. Kerkeslin was named by James Hector of the Palliser Expedition in 1859. It's a native word that means "wolverine." The mountain is 2984 m (9790 ft) high. An alpine valley glacier is concealed from view on its northern slopes.

44. **Athabasca Glacier**

Trailhead: Icefields Parkway (Highway 93), 127 km north from Lake Louise or 103 kilometres south from Jasper. Turn onto the Athabasca Glacier Road, 250 m south of the Icefield Centre. Follow this road 200 m to the first parking lot.
Rating: moderate, 2 km
Lighting: morning

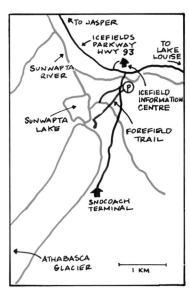

The Athabasca Glacier is the most accessible glacier in North America. Though many people drive to the parking lot closest to the glacier toe, the Forefield Trail allows a longer approach on foot. This rough trail has been cleared from glacial rubble, so wear sturdy footwear. If the day is typical, you will also need a warm hat, gloves, sweater, and windbreaker.

After crossing the forefield, the trail connects with the well-beaten path from the second parking lot to the toe of the glacier. For your safety, please keep to the path, and take heed of the warning (see box, p. 93).

The Athabasca Glacier is one of eight outlet valley glaciers that flow from Columbia Icefield. The glacier is 5.3 km long, 1 km wide, and contains an estimated 640 million cubic metres of ice. Impressive as these statistics may seem, they are but an inkling of the vast domain of ice that lies above in the Columbia Icefield.

Columbia Icefield

With an area of 230 sq km, Columbia Icefield is the largest in the Rockies. Nestled on an upland plateau with an average elevation of 3000 m (9840 ft), it is ringed by 13 of the 30 highest mountains in the Rockies. Meltwaters from the summit of Snow Dome flow to three oceans: the Pacific, the Atlantic, and the Arctic. The only other tri-oceanic apex in the world is in Siberia.

More than 10 m of snow falls on Columbia Icefield each year, and very little of this snow melts. Over time, the fallen snow changes shape from flakes to grains. Then the grains begin to compact under the weight of the snow layers above. Eventually, when about 30 m of compacted snow accumulates, the lower layers change into glacial ice. The maximum ice thickness on Columbia Icefield is approximately 365 m.

Columbia Icefield acts as a huge refrigerator, chilling the air mass above it. The cold air draining from the glacier will likely

make itself felt as you cross the forefield. This chill, coupled with the ever-changing courses of meltwater streams, makes it difficult for vegetation to grow nearby. Mats of white mountain avens, and clumps of snow willow, alpine willow, sedges, and mountain fireweed are all that have taken hold in half a century.

Glacier Movement

Glacial ice naturally flows down hill. Because it is under less resistance and pressure, ice on the surface of a glacier flows faster than ice at the base or sides. Glacial ice is also somewhat plastic and reacts to irregularities in the

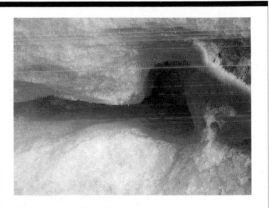

Colour of Glacial Ice

Ice on the surface of Athabasca Glacier appears white or gray because it contains air and other impurities that scatter the complete light spectrum back to the observer. Ice deep within a glacier may appear blue because air and other impurities have have been squeezed out of the ice. The compressed ice crystals have a uniform size and mainly reflect the blue wavelengths of light.

Photo opposite: The Athabasca Glacier flows from the Columbia Icefield to within 1.6 km of the Icefields Parkway. The Forefield Trail allows access to the glacier across an area that was covered by glacial ice less than a century ago.

Above: With an area of 230 sq km, the Columbia Icefield is the largest mass of permanent ice in the interior of North America. This is a mountaineer's view of the icefield, from the 3442 m (11,293 ft) summit of Mt. Andromeda.

bedrock beneath it. These properties create several surface features.

Crevasses (creh-VASS-es) are fissures in the surface of glacial ice. They can extend from side to side, or they can be parallel to the glacier's flow. Near the toe of the glacier, crevasses often splay out diagonally. It is estimated there are more than 30,000 crevasses on Athabasca Glacier. The jumble of crevasses towards the icefield rim mark the location of three icefalls, where the glacier drops over steps in the underlying bedrock.

Glacial Erosion

The tremendous pressure produced by the weight of ice gives awesome erosive power. Bedrock is shorn away, mountainsides are undercut and collapse, and the rock fragments are ground up. The resulting rock rubble, known to geologists as till, is the immediate product of glacial erosion. Glaciers incorporate till into their arsenal. Picked up and carried on the underside of the ice, rock fragments are dragged across the bedrock, catching in cracks, prying the rock apart and scouring it. Bedrock scratched in this fashion can be seen in the final approach to the Athabasca Glacier toe.

As an indicator of the quarrying going on beneath Athabasca Glacier, on a single hot, summer day, meltwater deposits 570 tonnes of rubble and silt into nearby Sunwapta Lake. As a result, this marginal lake, which the retreating ice uncovered in 1938, will soon be completely filled with debris.

Moraines

Although till is a product of destruction, glaciers create landforms from it called moraines. Lateral moraines are crested ridges that form alongside a glacier. The toe of Athabasca Glacier is flanked by wonderful examples. A terminal moraine is a horseshoe-shaped ridge created at the greatest advance of a glacier, and recessional moraines mark annual halting places during a period of retreat. The Forefield Trail cuts across a series of recessional moraines.

Global Warming

For millions of years, glacial ice has ebbed and flowed across much of the earth's surface. The most recent period of glacial advance was a relatively minor one known as the Little Ice Age, which lasted from approximately from 1200 A.D. to the late 1800s. Many glaciers have disappeared since that time. Others, like Athabasca Glacier, have shrunk considerably. What has caused this retreat? In a nutshell: global warming. The earth's climate has been warming during the last century and the glaciers are disappearing. The size of Athabasca Glacier is governed by two things: the amount of snow that falls annually on Columbia Icefield and the amount of snow or ice that melts annually from the glacier's surface. The glacier will advance when the winter snow accumulation exceeds the amount of summer melt. If melting exceeds accumulation, the glacier will retreat. Glacial retreat is a natural process. But there is concern that man's effect on the environment is contributing to unnatural global warming, and accelerating glacial retreat.

Glacial Retreat

How much does the Athabasca Glacier shrink each year? In recent years, the annual retreat has averaged one to three metres, measured lengthwise. Since 1870, the total retreat has been 1.6 km. As impressive as this retreat may seem, vertical shrinkage is also taking place. These losses are harder to gauge year-to-year, but over a long time they are staggering. It is estimated that the Athabasca Glacier decreased 57 percent in area and 32 percent in

volume between 1870 and 1971.

What does all this mean? Glaciers cover 11 percent of the world's surface and contain 75 percent of all freshwater as ice and snow. As glaciers melt this frozen reservoir is depleted. Some of the ice melting at the toe of Athabasca Glacier may have formed 800 years ago, before industrial pollution. Thus, melting glaciers represent the disappearance of nature's purest freshwater resources. At a time when demand for freshwater is increasing globally, the retreat of the world's glaciers becomes a vital concern.

Warning!

• Travel on glacier ice is for knowledgeable and equipped mountaineers only! The toe of Athabasca Glacier is very dangerous to the casual walker. The crevasses (slots in the ice) can be 30 m deep. Glacier ice is slippery. It is easy to lose your footing, especially during descent. If you fall into a crevasse you will be unable to climb out.

• Ice on a glacier's surface is very abrasive due to the high concentration of sediment. When you fall your skin will not be cut. Instead it will be torn away. Such injuries often become infected.

• As many people find out to their horror, even gentle ice slopes are much harder to descend than they are to ascend.

• What can you expect if you fall into a crevasse? Quick rescue is doubtful. Death awaits most people who fall into crevasses unroped. Hypothermia, injuries sustained in the fall, and drowning are the major causes of death. **Stay off the ice!**

45. **Wilcox Pass**

Trailhead: Wilcox
Creek Campground
on the Icefields
Parkway (Hwy 93),
(2.8 km south of the
Icefield Centre; 124
km north of Lake
Louise)
Rating: harder,
4.5 km
Lighting: morning

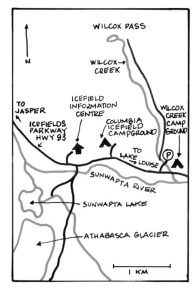

From the Wilcox Pass trail the hiker obtains an overview of the high mountains and spectacular glaciers on the northeast edge of Columbia Icefield. This historic trail climbs steadily to alpine tundra, the haunt of bighorn sheep and grizzly bear. Dress warmly!

When the first travellers ventured north from Lake Louise in the 1890s, Athabasca Glacier blocked the valley that now contains the Icefields Parkway. Rather than crossing the glacial ice with horses and tackling a narrow canyon beyond, the outfitters detoured over an alpine pass, and regained the Sunwapta Valley at Tangle Creek. The pass and mountain are named after Walter Wilcox, the first explorer to make this detour

At the outset, the trail enters an old-growth forest dominated by Engelmann spruce. The larger trees are more than 400 years old, nearly a metre in diameter, and 20 metres tall – remarkable considering the severity of the local climate. The stumps in the first few hundred metres are of trees cut for bridge timbers during construction of the original Icefields Parkway.

After a steep climb, the trail levels out on a cliff edge overlooking the Icefields Parkway and the Athabasca Glacier area. The mountain nearest you is Mt. Athabasca. Behind it is Mt. Andromeda. Look for climbers – tiny, black specks on the expansive glaciers and icy faces of these mountains. West of Athabasca Glacier, the spectacular Dome Glacier cascades from the icefield rim, between Snow Dome and Mt. Kitchener.

Resume the moderate climb towards Wilcox Pass. You may encounter the resident band of bighorn sheep. The mountain on your east (right) is Nigel Peak, named for Nigel Vavasour, camp cook on the mountaineering expedition that discovered Columbia Icefield in 1898.

A further 2 km of delightful hiking across alpine tundra leads to the expansive, boggy summit area

of Wilcox Pass, elevation 2375 m (7792 ft). A large rock cairn generally serves as the turnaround point. There is a variety of wildflowers in Wilcox Pass. The pass is frequented by grizzly bear and occasionally moose. Look for a golden eagle overhead.

Photo opposite: The Wilcox Pass trail was built in the 1890s to bypass the Athabasca Glacier, when it blocked travel in the Sunwapta Valley. Here you can see Athabasca and Dome glaciers.

Grizzly Bear

The grizzly bear is king of the food chain in the Rockies. Although a formidable animal, in the Rockies it is not a great hunter – 90 percent of its diet is vegetarian. Berries and roots are the main foods. Grizzlies range from valley bottom to mountaintop, feeding at low elevations in spring and autumn, and higher in the summer. They spend the months of November to April hibernating in dens dug into steep mountainsides. The adult male grizzly is 1.3 m tall at the shoulder, and can weigh more than 300 kg. The smaller female breeds every other year. She gives birth to cubs (usually twins) in the den. Colour and size are not the best way to distinguish between grizzly and black bears. Look for the grizzly's prominent shoulder hump and dished face. "Grizzly" refers not to the bear's disposition, but to its grayish-tipped coat. It is estimated there are 180 to 220 grizzlies in Banff and Jasper national parks.

OTHER WALKS AND HIKES IN JASPER NATIONAL PARK

See map on page 67

46. Stanley Falls

Trailhead: Icefields Parkway (Highway 93), 15 km north of the Icefield Centre; 88 km south of Jasper. Look for the small parking area with a hiker symbol on the east side of the highway.
Rating: moderate, 2.5 km
Lighting: afternoon

After crossing a drainage dike adjacent to the Icefields Parkway, the Stanley Falls trail cuts through a narrow section of forest. When you emerge from this, turn right onto the old roadbed, abandoned when the Parkway was upgraded in the late 1950s. At the mouth of Beauty Creek, a rough track veers left and follows the rim of a picturesque canyon which contains eight waterfalls. Stanley Falls is the last and the highest of these. Always in the shade, it is difficult to photograph. However, some of the cascades in the lower canyon are quite photogenic. This trail is sometimes used by mountain caribou.

47. Sunwapta Falls and Canyon

Trailhead: Icefields Parkway (Highway 93), 48 km north of the Icefield Centre; 55 km south of Jasper. Follow the Sunwapta Falls Road 1 km to the parking lot.
Rating: Viewpoint. Wheelchair accessible
Lighting: afternoon

At Sunwapta Falls, the Sunwapta River has been diverted from its former course by a glacial moraine. In following its newer path, the river has eroded a crack system in the underlying limestone to create the falls, as well as four other cascades in a canyon further downstream. This lower canyon is reached by a 2 km walk along the near bank, through open lodgepole pine forest. On the way, mountains near the headwaters of the Athabasca River are visible.

48. Buck, Honeymoon, and Osprey Lakes

Trailhead: Icefields Parkway, 50 km north of the Icefield Centre; 53 km south of Jasper
Rating: easy, 1.5 km
Lighting: anytime

Buck Lake is 250 m straight ahead from the parking area. About half way to Buck Lake, the trail to Honeymoon and Osprey Lakes branches north (left). It reaches the south shore of Honeymoon Lake, before heading east through a black spruce bog to Osprey Lake. Wear rubber boots! Orchids grow at trailside, and moose and osprey are among wildlife you may see in the area.

When glacial ice last receded from the floor of the Athabasca Valley, large blocks of ice became detached, and melted into the rubble. The lakes that resulted are known as kettle ponds. These three lakes are examples.

49. **Wabasso Lake**

Trailhead: Icefields Parkway (Highway 93), 87 km north of the Icefield Centre; 16 km south of Jasper
Rating: moderate, 2.7 km
Lighting: anytime

Wabasso is a seldom visited lake in the rolling gritstone ridge country of the Athabasca Valley. The name is a native word for "rabbit." The trail ambles up and down over a series of ridges, and at Km 1.5, skirts a slough created by beavers. Keep left at all trail junctions. After climbing over another ridge, the trail drops to a picturesque cascade that drains the marshes below Wabasso Lake. The lake is reached in a further 700 m. Although views are limited, the Maligne Range from Mt. Tekarra to Mt. Hardisty is visible. Osprey nest at the lake. Keep right at all junctions on your return.

50. **Lac Beauvert**

Trailheads: Start at the boathouse at Jasper Park Lodge.
Or take Highway 93A south from the corner of Hazel Avenue and Connaught Drive in Jasper townsite. Cross Highway 16. Turn east (left) onto the Lac Beauvert Road and cross the Athabasca River. Follow the road to the Lac Beauvert parking lot.
Rating: moderate, 3.2 km loop
Lighting: anytime

Lac Beauvert is French for "beautiful green lake." A circuit of this horseshoe-shaped lake makes an ideal family outing. Jasper Park Lodge originated in 1922. Earlier accommodation at the site included a camp called "Tent City," and possibly Henry House, a fur trade outpost. As the trail skirts the north and west shores of the lake, it passes through open forest and grasslands, which are important year-round range for elk. Loon and Canada geese are common summer residents on the lake. The circuit is completed along walkways on the lodge's golf course, on the south side of the lake.

51. **Cottonwood Slough**

Trailhead: Pyramid Stables on the Pyramid Lake Road, 4 km north of Jasper
Rating: easy, 1.5 km
Lighting: afternoon and evening

There is a maze of hiking trails on the Pyramid Bench north of Jasper townsite. Unfortunately, due to excessive use by horses, most of these trails are in poor condition, and cannot be recommended. Because it has better drained soils underfoot, the trail to Cottonwood Slough (SLEW) is the best the area offers.

From the stables, take Trail #6 which begins across the Pyramid Lake Road. After 150 m, take the left fork in the trail. In another 300 m, branch right. As it gains the banks above the first pond in the slough, the trail breaks out of pine and aspen forest onto a dry, grassy south-facing slope, topped by ancient Douglas firs. When the second pond comes into view, a spur trail branches downhill to allow a closer look. There is a large beaver lodge in this pond, and the area is good for bird-watching.

52. **Beaver Lake**

Trailhead: Follow Highway 16, for 3.7 km east of Jasper to the Maligne Lake Road. Turn east (right) and follow the Maligne Lake Road 28 km to the Beaver Creek picnic area at the far end of Medicine Lake.
Rating: easy, 1.6 km
Lighting: afternoon

The short walk north to Beaver Lake is along the Jacques Lake trail, a wide, well-graded road bed, ideal for families. The beautiful, glacial waters of the lake reflect the steeply tilted sawtooth mountains of the Queen Elizabeth Range.

53. **Mona, Lorraine, and Moose Lakes**

Trailheads: Follow Highway 16, for 3.7 km east from Jasper to the Maligne Lake Road. Turn east (right) and follow this road 45 km to its end at the parking lot on the west side of Maligne Lake. There are two trailheads with signs, next to this parking lot. The trailhead for Mona and Lorraine lakes is the Skyline Trail. The Moose Lake Trail begins at the Bald Hills trailhead.
Ratings: Mona Lake, moderate 2.4 km; Lorraine Lake, moderate 2.1 km; and Moose Lake, easy 2.4 km loop
Lighting: anytime.

The rockslide which dammed Maligne Lake was so colossal, it spread completely across the valley floor. Small lakes now fill the depressions in the rockslide debris. To reach Mona and Lorraine lakes, hike the Skyline Trail through open pine forest to the spur trails that lead south (left) to Lorraine Lake, and north (right) to Mona Lake. These lakes were named for two of Jasper's first female trail guides.

To reach Moose Lake, take the Bald Hills Trail and then branch south (left) at the first junction (300 m). Walk another kilometre, then turn east (left) to the shores of Moose Lake. From the lake's north shore, a trail returns to Maligne Lake. The parking lot is then easily reached by walking north.

54. **Miette Boardwalk and Hot Springs**

Trailhead: Follow Highway 16 east of Jasper, 42.9 km to the Miette Hot Springs Road. Turn south (right) and follow this road 19 km to its end at the Miette Hot Springs parking lot.
Rating: easy, 800 m
Lighting: anytime

From the hot springs parking lot, walk south on the road across Sulphur Creek, to the old hot springs building. Constructed in 1937, this building saw service until deemed unsafe in 1984. The boardwalk beyond the old building leads to outlets of the springs, the hottest and most pungent in the Rockies.

YOHO NATIONAL PARK

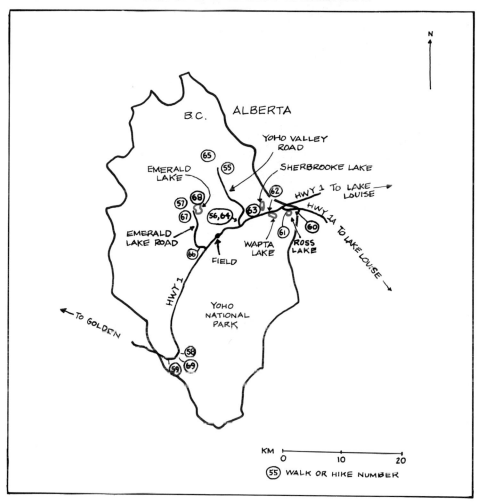

Yoho is a native expression of "awe and wonder." Yoho National Park was established in 1886 as Canada's second national park. Though one of the smallest of the Rocky Mountain national parks, Yoho's landscape has tremendous variety. The park's theme is "rockwalls and waterfalls."

The eastern part of the park features: glaciers, icefields, lakes, and the high peaks of the Continental Divide. The drier, warmer western area of the park features the broad valley of the Kicking Horse River and abundant wildlife. The park's other attractions are a rich human history and the soft-bodied fossils of the Burgess Shale.

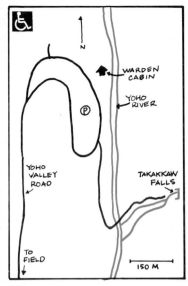

55. Takakkaw Falls

Photo above: Yoho National Park's theme is "rockwalls and waterfalls." Fittingly, Takakkaw Falls, third highest in Canada, is the park's emblem. The falls are fed by meltwater from the Waputik Icefield.

Trailhead: Follow Highway 1 to the Yoho Valley Road, 3.7 km east of Field; 22.3 km west of Lake Louise. Trailers and large recreational vehicles should be left at the trailer drop off.Follow the Yoho Valley Road 14 km to its end at the Takakkaw Falls parking lot.

Rating: easy, 600 m. Wheelchair accessible

Lighting: afternoon

At a surveyed height of 378 m (1247 ft), Takakkaw (TAH-kuh-kah) Falls is one of the most impressive road-side views in the Rockies. More than any other walk or hike in Yoho, the paved trail to the base of the falls best displays the park's theme: "rock walls and water-falls."

Takakkaw is a Cree expression meaning "it is wonderful." The first recorded visit to the falls was in 1897, by German explorer Jean Habel (AHH-bull). Habel's ac-count of the wonders he saw was instrumental in expanding the original 16 sq km Mt. Stephen Reserve in 1901.

The Yoho Valley Road is not plowed between October and June. And snow and avalanche debris may remain at roadside throughout the summer. At one point the road switchbacks sharply to bypass a canyon. Buses cannot turn in the tight radius, and must reverse along the middle switchback. Look for mountain goats, porcupines and hoary marmots during the drive.

The amount of water in Takakkaw Falls varies with the season and time of day. It will be at maximum on hot afternoons in July and August. Boulders carried in the stream's flow can often be heard tumbling down the cliff. Visitors in late afternoon or early evening may see a rainbow in the falls on sunny days.

In winter, the volume of the falls is reduced to a trickle. A broad shield of ice forms lower down, with a series of narrow pillars higher up. The frozen falls were first climbed in 1974, heralding the arrival of waterfall ice climbing as a significant winter activity in the Rockies.

The mountains immediately above Takakkaw Falls are part of the Waputik (WAH-poo-tick) Range. Waputik is a Stoney word for "white goat." Mountain goats are frequently seen at the base of the cliffs near the falls. For many years Takakkaw Falls was touted as "the highest waterfall in Canada." Howerver, measuring the height of waterfalls is an imprecise art, and there is argument as to whether all, or only the largest cascade should be included. It is now generally agreed Takakkaw is third highest in Canada. First is Della Falls on Vancouver Island, followed by Hunlen Falls in Tweedsmuir Park, B.C.

Glacial ice eroded the U-shaped trough of the Yoho Valley more deeply than its tributary valleys. So the mouths of these side valleys have been left hanging above the main valley floor. As a result, the Yoho is a valley of waterfalls. No less than eight cascades mark the locations where side valley streams plunge into the main valley. Today, the Yoho Glacier, architect of this valley, is only a remnant of its former self. It has receded to the edge of the 40 sq km Wapta Icefield. The Yoho Glacier may be seen from several places along the Yoho Valley Road.

What's above the Takakkaw Falls?

The landscape above Takakkaw Falls is one of the most spectacular in the Rockies. The water that feeds the falls empties from a marginal lake at the toe of Daly Glacier, one of five outlet valley glaciers of the 32 sq km Waputik Icefield. This photograph shows a mountaineer's view of the lake, glacier, and Mt. Balfour – highest mountain in the area. Hikers may obtain a distant view of this scene from the Yoho Pass and Iceline trails, on the opposite side of the Yoho Valley.

56. A Walk in the Past

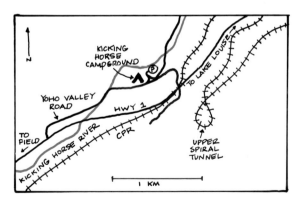

KICKING
HORSE
CAMPGROUND

N

TO LAKE LOUISE

YOHO VALLEY
ROAD

HWY 1

TO
FIELD

KICKING HORSE RIVER

CPR

UPPER
SPIRAL
TUNNEL

1 KM

Trailhead: Follow Highway 1 to the Yoho Valley Road, 3.7 km east of Field; 22.3 km west of Lake Louise. Take the Yoho Valley Road 1 km to Kicking Horse Campground. Enter the campground and drive to the interpretive theatre parking area. The trail begins at the display nearby.

Rating: moderate, 1.2 km. brochure available at trailhead

Lighting: anytime

The six interpretive stops along A Walk in the Past explore the history of the Canadian Pacific Railway (CPR) at the bottom of Yoho's notorious "Big Hill."

After crossing the Yoho Valley Road, the trail ascends towards the CPR main line, through a damp, shaded forest featuring western red cedar. Beside the double set of railway tracks are deposits of coal soot and cinders. These accumulated during the 70 years of coal-fired railway operations that preceded the arrival of the diesel age in 1956. Please use caution crossing the rails. Watch for oil and grease underfoot.

Across the tracks, the trail crosses the original railway grade, abandoned when the Spiral Tunnels were completed. Later, this grade was part of the Kicking Horse Trail, a road completed from Lake Louise to Golden in 1927. A short climb leads to a gravel road and Stop #5. Turn right and follow the road 200 m, before veering left on a trail to the last stop on this walk.

The CPR's contract with the government required the grade of the railway not to exceed 2.2 percent. So, the original grade, surveyed through the steep ravine on the west side of Kicking Horse Pass, would have required many tunnels to complete. However, the CPR could not afford the time or expense of constructing the railway to specifications. Hence, General Manager, William Cornelius Van Horne, adopted a "temporary solution" – and ran the rails straight down the hill in 1884. At a grade of 4.48 percent, this section of line was the steepest ever used on a regularly operated commercial railway, anywhere in the world.

The horrors and headaches of the Big Hill plagued the CPR for 25 years. Four, 150 tonne locomotives were required to push a 14 car, 700 tonne freight train up the hill. The 14 km trip took an hour. The wear and tear on equipment created tremendous, unforeseen expense. Scheduling, rather an imprecise art for a trans-continental railway in the late 1800s, produced mayhem. Trains frequently stalled going uphill, and ranaway coming down, sometimes derailing with loss of life. In addition, avalanches and washouts occured.

However, the completion of the Spiral Tunnels in 1909 helped alleviate these problems. The two ingeniously constructed tunnels combine to add nearly 7 km to the length of the railway line, but reduced the grade to 2.2 percent. Two locomotives could now do the work of four. Construction of the tunnels cost 1.5 million dollars, required the efforts of 1000 workers, and consumed 700,000 kg of dynamite.

Photo opposite: A narrow gauge locomotive at work on the "Big Hill," during construction of the Spiral Tunnels, 1908-09. Photo by R.B. Molyneux, courtesy of the Glenbow Archive (Calgary).

The End of the Line

During construction of the Spiral Tunnels, two narrow gauge locomotives were used to haul away rubble. When the tunnels were completed, one of the locomotives was sold. The other was abandoned. Today, the last stop on A Walk in the Past visits the well-preserved remains of this locomotive, built in 1885.

Locomotives were the workhorses on Yoho's "Big Hill" in the late 1800s. However, they were dangerous to operate on the mountain section of the Canadian Pacific Railway. They sometimes "ran away" and derailed coming down the hill, killing workers. After one such engine was repaired, it exploded while going up the hill, killing three people.

57. **Emerald Lake**

Trailhead: Follow Highway 1 to the Emerald Lake Road, 2.6 km west of Field. Turn right, and follow the road 8 km to its end at the Emerald Lake parking lot. The trailhead is to the west (left) of the bridge.
Rating: moderate, 4.8 km loop. Wheelchair accessible for 2 km
Lighting: anytime

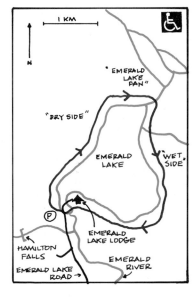

The Emerald Lake circuit is one of the most enjoyable nature walks in the Rockies and displays diverse vegetation. The first 500 m of trail is paved, and wheelchair access is possible for a further 1.5 km. Walk the circuit in a clockwise direction, and keep right at all trail junctions.

With an area of 116 hectares (287 acres), Emerald Lake is the largest in Yoho. Emerald Lake occupies a glacier-scoured hollow and has a maximum depth of 28 m. The outlet has been dammed by a glacial moraine. The lake's surface is frozen from late November to early May.

Rainbow trout, cutthroat trout, eastern brook trout, and slimy sculpin are the recorded fish species in Emerald Lake. Several pairs of common loon and a pair of osprey usually reside at the lake during summer. In spring and autumn, the waters are sometimes used as a stopover by Canada geese.

In your walk around Emerald Lake, you will notice marked changes in the vegetation. The lake is frequently described as having a "dry side" and a "wet side." The "wet side" includes the east and south shores that lie at the base of shaded mountain slopes. The upper parts of these slopes hold snow most of the summer, and also receive a lot of rain. The cool, damp environment allows growth of a lush forest. The "dry side" is normal for its location. It is only "dry" relative to the "wet side."

The Dry Side

The forest on the west or "dry side" of the lake contains subalpine fir and white spruce. This habitat suits the Clark's nutcracker, gray jay, red squirrel, and American marten. In the undergrowth, Labrador tea and buffaloberry are common shrubs. Pink wintergreen, arnica, dwarf dogwood, and yellow columbine are attractive wildflowers.

The Avalanche Path

Five hundred metres from the trailhead, the trail crosses a large avalanche path, where snow avalanches from the upper slopes of Emerald Peak sweep the mountainside each winter and spring. The supple willows and

Photo opposite: Emerald Lake is the largest lake in Yoho National Park. Pioneer guide and outfitter Tom Wilson discovered it in 1882, the same year he discovered Lake Louise.

Devil's Club

Ask any mountaineer to name the plant with the worst reputation in British Columbia. "Devil's club" will invariably be the answer. Growing in the damp undergrowth of cedar rainforest, this tall (up to 3 m) shrub has a natural armour capable of inflicting great pain: the succulent stem is covered in sharp spines that cause inflammation of the skin. The huge, maple-like leaves are also fringed underneath with spines. Devil's club adds insult to injury. Brush against it after a rain, and it will give you a good soaking too. Mountaineers in the Rockies are fortunate that this plant grows mainly in the isolated wet belts, at low elevation on the western slopes. Despite its poor reputation, devil's club in fruit is beautiful to behold. Its white flowers yield shiny red berries, which sit upright atop the stem. Look, but don't touch!

alders that grow here are favourite foods of moose.

In the view southeast from the avalanche slope, the peak directly behind Emerald Lake Lodge is Mt. Burgess. This view was featured on the Canadian ten dollar bill from 1954 to 1971. To the left of Mt. Burgess is Mt. Field, and farther left is Wapta Mountain. It was here in 1909, on the ridge connecting these last two mountains, that Charles Walcott of the Smithsonian Institution discovered the 530 million-year-old soft-bodied fossils in the Burgess Shale. The site later became known as the Walcott Quarry. Research continues every summer.

Beyond the avalanche path, the character of the forest changes frequently. There are drier areas of lodgepole pine and Douglas fir, and damper places with western yew and western red cedar.

The Emerald Fan

After passing some springs in the lake bottom and a horse/hiker barrier, the trail swings east (right) onto an alluvial fan, created from rubble carried by glacial melt streams. Because of rocky soils, cold air, the ever-changing courses of the streams, and the high water table under the stream gravels, it is difficult for vegetation to grow on the fan. Trees include lodgepole pine and gnarled white spruce. Juniper and willows grow beneath them.

In summer, the alluvial fan can be transformed from icebox to furnace. On sunny and calm days, soaring temperatures and intense light result when sunlight reflects off the rocks. Many of the mat-like plants are pale on the undersides of their leaves, in order to reflect the light and heat. On windy days trees are exposed to the full brunt of winds from across the lake. Some of the trees near the lakeshore "flag" the prevailing southwest wind, by growing branches only on their northeast sides.

As harsh as the environment on the alluvial fan sounds, nature decorates it with wildflowers. Mats of yellow mountain avens, bearberry, and twinflower are found in the drier areas. The wetter areas support sedge meadows, blue-eyed grass, cotton grass, and a variety of orchids, including: yellow lady's slipper, tall white bog orchid, and hooded lady's tresses. White camas and Indian paintbrush are common at trailside.

Looking south across the lake from the fan, the horn mountain shapes of the Van Horne Range are prominent. These mountains were named for William Cornelius Van Horne, vice-president and general manager of the CPR during its construction. The highest peak is Mt. King, with a small niche glacier on its north slope.

The Delta

The bridge at the far side of the fan crosses one of the main inlets to the lake. This stream deposits fine sediments that build a delta. Emerald Lake is one of a few places in the Rockies where a delta and an alluvial fan are found together. Pondweed, horsetail, and sedges grow here, providing cover for waterfowl and food for moose.

The Wet Side

Across the bridge, the forest immediately becomes more dense. Welcome to the wet side of the lake. Here you find tree species more typical of coastal rainforest than the Rockies. Shrub-like western red cedar are interspersed among ancient white spruce, subalpine fir, and a few western hemlock and Douglas fir. Hot forest fires have been absent from this shore of the lake for several hundred years, allowing this "old-growth" forest to develop. In the undergrowth, green alder, ferns, thimbleberry, devil's club, horsetails, queen's cup, and foam flower are common. After you pass the Burgess Pass junction, scan the lakeshore for moose. Use caution on the boardwalks. The wood is often slippery.

Emerald Lake Lodge

The Emerald Lake circuit finishes in a short climb to the crest of the moraine that dams the lake. This pile of glacial rubble was deposited at the end of the Wisconsin Glaciation, 11,000 years ago. Emerald Lake Lodge has been constructed on top of this moraine. The main lodge building includes part of the original chalet constructed by the CPR in 1902. The lodge was completely redeveloped in 1985-86.

To reach the parking lot, walk through the lodge grounds to the bridge at the lake's outlet. To the north, across the waters are the massive, glacier-capped cliffs of The Vice President (named for the vice-president of the CPR). To the south, Mt. Burgess is reflected in the lagoon that has formed behind the moraine. Barn swallows provide constant aerial entertainment and fish rise occasionally from below. In the evening, the bridge is a good place to watch the rapid comings and goings of little brown bats. They swoop over the lake, feeding on insects. During daytime, they congregate under the eaves of the lodge.

Yellow Lady's Slipper

Easily recognized, the orchid, yellow lady's slipper, is one of the most beautiful wildflowers in the Rockies. The pouch-like slipper hangs slightly from a stem which is 20 to 30 cm in height. The interior of the pouch features purple highlights. This flower grows in damp areas of shaded woods and occasionally on open gravel close to water, as at the "Emerald Fan." It blooms from mid-June to mid-July.

Although yellow lady's slipper can be locally common, picking the flower will kill the plant, resulting in its disappearance. Please leave this beautiful flower for others to enjoy.

58. **Leanchoil Hoodoos**

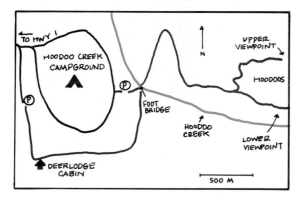

There are two starting points for the hike to the Leanchoil (lee-ANN-coil) Hoodoos. The route from the Deerlodge trailhead offers an opportunity for a quick side trip to Deerlodge cabin, the first warden patrol cabin built in Yoho (see p. 114). Beyond the cabin, the trail circles to the rear of the campground, through a damp forest of lodgepole pine and white spruce. The trail emerges after 1.5 km at the footbridge across Hoodoo Creek. Those staying in the campground may choose to begin the hike here.

Trailhead: Follow Highway 1 for 22.6 km west of Field to the Hoodoo Creek Campground. Turn left and follow the campground road 600 m to a junction.

Turn right on a gravel road, and follow this 400 m to the Deerlodge / Hoodoos trailhead. When the campground is closed (Sept. to June), you may have

to park at the gate on the campground road and walk to the trailhead.
Rating: harder, 3.1 km
Lighting: anytime

It is only 1.6 km from the Hoodoo Creek bridge to the upper viewpoint at the hoodoos. However, the trail gains 450 m of elevation in that distance. With an average grade of roughly 30 percent, this is by far the steepest hike in this book. Please keep to the trail, and avoid shortcutting the corners. There is no drinking water beyond the footbridge.

From the footbridge the initial climb is on a dry, south-facing sideslope at the mouth of the creek. This is perfect soil and exposure for Douglas fir. Large, fire-scarred specimens of this tree are prominent at trailside. Soon the trail swings into the Hoodoo Creek valley. In places you will be exposed to a steep drop. Use caution.

The cool, moist air channelled along the creek produces a marked transition in the forest about a kilometre from the foot bridge. The Douglas firs give way to subalpine fir, white spruce, and lodgepole pine. Feather mosses cover the forest floor, along with the wildflowers, dwarf dogwood and queen's cup. Calypso orchids bloom here in June.

At the trail junction, those who are tired may want to take the right fork to the lower viewpoint. For the best view, take the left fork to the upper viewpoint. This section of trail is the steepest, but the view is worth the effort. A small bench above the hoodoos marks the end of trail. The lofty mountain rising behind the hoodoos is Chancellor Peak.

Most of the Leanchoil Hoodoos are topped by capstones that have protected the columns from erosion as the surrounding till weathered away.

Leanchoil is a Scottish name connected with the construction of the Canadian Pacific Railway. The mother of Donald Smith, a CPR stockholder, lived in a Scottish manor named Leth-na-Coyle. The name was applied to a nearby railway siding just west of here in 1884.

Photo opposite: The Leanchoil Hoodoos were created by the same process as those near Tunnel Mountain Campground (Banff). Unlike the Tunnel Mountain Hoodoos, most of the Leanchoil Hoodoos are topped with capstones.

Tree Lichens

The branches of many trees in the damp forest along Hoodoo Creek are covered in hair-like growths commonly called "Spanish moss" or "old man's beard." These growths are not moss; they are tree lichens. Lichens are a sophisticated vegetation, in which a fungus and an algae coexist. The fungus provides shelter for the algae; and the algae produces food for both.

Some of the more common tree lichens are the greenish *Usnea* (see photo) and *Allectoria;* the black *Bryoria;* and the brilliant green wolf lichen. Further north in the Rockies, these plants are a vital food source for mountain caribou.

59. **Wapta Falls**

Photo above: At Wapta Falls, the Kicking Horse River plunges over a 30 m ledge that spans the width of the river. At times the roar of the falls is audible for more than 2 km.

Trailhead: Follow Highway 1, for 24.7 km west of Field. Turn south (left) onto the Wapta Falls road and follow it 1.6 km to the trailhead.
Rating: moderate, 2.4 km
Lighting: anytime

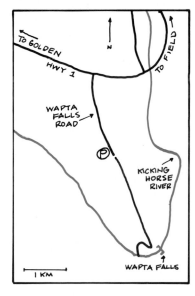

The Wapta Falls Trail is ideal for a family outing. It travels through a pleasant forest to the waterfall, a 30m high ledge that spans the Kicking Horse River.

The initial kilometre of trail is along the edge of a clearing originally intended for a road. The trail narrows as it enters a dense forest and a short climb leads to a viewpoint above the falls. For a closer view of the falls, continue downhill on the trail 400 m to the gravel beach. The outcrops in the river mark former locations of the falls.

The open montane forest here is typical of the drier low elevations in southwestern Yoho National Park. White spruce, lodgepole pine, cottonwood poplar, and trembling aspen are the most common trees. Black bear, ruffed grouse, and white-tailed deer are sometimes seen.

In August 1858, a party from the Palliser Expedition explored the central Rockies. Led by James Hector, a Scottish doctor and geologist, the men eventually reached the confluence of the Beaverfoot and Kicking Horse rivers above Wapta Falls. While struggling with a pack horse, Hector was kicked in the chest by the horse and rendered unconscious. His men assumed he was dead and were preparing to bury him, when to their mutual surprise, Hector revived. Although injured and in great pain, Hector was on his horse again the next day as the party headed east towards the Continental Divide. In his journal James Hector remarked that his men now called the river "The Kicking Horse." Previous to that time it had been known by the native name *wapta*, which means "river".

The Kicking Horse is the largest river in Yoho National Park, and drains virtually the entire park area of 1313 sq km. At Wapta Falls, the peak volume has been measured at 255 cubic metres of flow per second. The Kicking Horse was designated a Canadian Heritage River in 1989.

Wapta Falls have been cut through an outcrop of the 500-million-year-old shale of the McKay (muck-EYE) Formation. Before the Wisconsin Glaciation, it is thought that the Kicking Horse River flowed south into what is now Kootenay National Park. After that ice age, a moraine blocked the southerly course of the river, diverting it west where it found a weakness in the shale and created the falls. Captured by a lower valley, the river then eroded a canyon northwest to Golden.

Bearberry

The evergreen shrub, bearberry, is one of the most common plants in the ground cover of the montane ecoregion. It grows as a trailing vine and forms mats on dry slopes. The delicate, urn-shaped flowers bloom in early summer. They are white with pink edging and hang downwards from the stem. Glossy red berries replace the flowers by August. As the plant's name suggests, these berries are a favourite food of black bears.

Bearberry is also known as kinnikinnik (KINNY-kin-ick), which means "a mixture which is smoked." Natives made a kind of tobacco from its dried leaves, fruits and bark. Bearberry is a member of the heath family that includes blueberries and mountain heather (see p. 85). There are three bearberry species in the Rockies. Two of them occur at higher elevations.

OTHER WALKS AND HIKES IN YOHO NATIONAL PARK

See map on page 99

60. The Great Divide

Trailhead: Banff / Yoho national park boundary on Highway 1A, 3 km east of its junction with Highway 1 in Yoho National Park; 10.7 km west of Lake Louise Village
Rating: viewpoint. Wheelchair accessible
Lighting: anytime

The Great Divide, in Kicking Horse Pass, marks the point where Divide Creek branches. One fork flows east into Alberta and the other flows west into British Columbia. This tiny creek sends waters to both the Atlantic and Pacific oceans, and forms the boundary between two provinces and two national parks. The interpretive displays highlight the differences between the eastern and western slopes of the Rockies, and they describe the activities of the Interprovincial Boundary Survey from 1913 to1925. A cairn commemorates explorer James Hector, who discovered Kicking Horse Pass in 1858.

61. Ross Lake

Trailhead: Highway 1A, 1 km west of The Great Divide; 11.7 km west of Lake Louise Village; 2 km east of the junction with Highway 1. The trail begins opposite a small parking area.
Rating: moderate, 1.2 km
Lighting: afternoon

Ross Lake is a glacial tarn, scoured from the bedrock by a glacier that once flowed from the hanging valley above. The lake is reached by a pleasant walk through subalpine forest, along an old logging road south from Highway 1A. The picturesque lake is backed by 400-metre high limestone cliffs, home to a band of mountain goats. Ross Lake was named for James Ross, a railway construction boss.

62. Sherbrooke Lake

Trailhead: Follow Highway 1, 11 km east of Field; 15 km west of Lake Louise Village
Rating: harder, 2.8 km
Lighting: morning and afternoon

The Sherbrooke Lake Trail gains 190 metres of elevation from Highway 1 through subalpine forest to the shores of a picturesque lake, nestled between Mt. Ogden and Paget Peak. In the vicinity of the lake there are many wildflowers, including species of orchids. The waters have the blue-green hue of a glacial lake. Mt. Niles is the prominent peak beyond the head of the lake.

63. Spiral Tunnel Viewpoint

Trailhead: Follow Highway 1, 7.4 km east of Field; 18.6 km west of Lake Louise Village
Rating: viewpoint. Wheelchair accessible
Lighting: morning and afternoon

The original line of the CPR descended the Big Hill from Wapta Lake to Field directly – a grade of 4.48 percent. Wrecks occurred frequently when trains "ranaway." In 1909, the two Spiral Tunnels were completed, adding 7 km to the length of the line, and reducing the grade to 2.2 percent. One thousand workers and 700,000 tonnes of dynamite were required in the construction. The lower

Spiral Tunnel in Mt. Ogden is visible from this viewpoint. Some 30 trains a day pass through the tunnels, so have patience if you wish to see a train loop over itself. The Yoho Valley is in view to the north.

64. **Centennial Trail**

Trailhead: Follow Highway 1 to the Yoho Valley Road (3.7 km east of Field; 22.3 km west of Lake Louise). Follow this road to the first bridge over the Kicking Horse River (100 m west of Kicking Horse Campground.) The trail is on the west side of the bridge and follows the river upstream to the north.
Rating: easy, 2.5 km loop
Lighting: anytime

The Centennial Trail was constructed to commemorate the national parks centennial in 1985. It follows the Kicking Horse River and crosses a prominent avalanche slope on Mt. Field. In spring 1989, an avalanche from this slope swept across the river, damaging some facilities in the campground. Look for mountain goats on the cliffs above. Across the valley, the cliffs of Mts. Field and Stephen feature mine portals, used during the heyday of the Monarch and Kicking Horse mines. Lead, silver, and zinc were the minerals sought. Mining ended in 1952.

Where the trail rejoins the road, turn south (right), cross the bridge, leave the road, and follow the gravel path into the campground.

65. **Laughing Falls**

Trailhead: Follow Highway 1 to the Yoho Valley Road (3.7 km east of Field; 22.3 km west of Lake Louise). Leave trailers and large recreational vehicles at the trailer drop off. Follow the Yoho Valley road 14 km to the end at the Takakkaw Falls parking lot. Drive through the main parking lot to a smaller parking lot located on the right. Walk through the campground to the Yoho Valley trailhead.
Rating: harder, 4.7 km
Lighting: morning

The original carriage road in the Yoho Valley was completed in 1910, and led beyond Takakkaw Falls. Hence the first section of this trail, across alluvial fan and through subalpine forest, is road width. (Sidetrips at km 2.6 lead to Angel's Staircase and Point Lace Falls). Between km 2.6 and km. 4, the main trail then narrows and climbs steeply. At km 4, a short side trail leads left to Duchesnay Lake. The main trail crosses the Little Yoho River to Laughing Falls Campground just downstream from Laughing Falls. The falls are reached by walking a short distance west from the campground, along the north bank of the Little Yoho River. On sunny days, early morning visitors may see a rainbow in the spray.

66. **Natural Bridge**

Trailhead: Follow Highway 1 to the Emerald Lake Road (2.6 km west of Field). Turn north (right), and follow the road 1.5 km. Turn left into a paved parking area.
Rating: viewpoint. Wheelchair accessible
Lighting: afternoon

Natural Bridge marks the point where the Kicking Horse River encounters a relatively resistant limestone outcrop in an area of otherwise weak shales. Formerly, the river cascaded over the lip of the limestone step as a waterfall, but over time it has eroded downwards into a crack behind the lip, creating the bridge. At high water the Kicking Horse River flows completely over the bridge.

67. **Hamilton Falls**

Trailhead: Follow Highway 1 to the Emerald Lake Road (2.6 km west of Field). Turn north (right), and follow the road 8 km to its end at the Emerald Lake parking lot. The trailhead is at the southwest corner of the parking lot.
Rating: easy, 800 m
Lighting: morning

Hamilton Falls cascade over a limestone cliff at the shaded base of Mt. Carnarvon. The trail features vegetation normally found on the Pacific coast including western red cedar. Bunchberry, thimbleberry, foam plant, queen's cup, and ferns dominate the undergrowth. Part of the old water collection system for Emerald Lake Lodge is visible at the base of the falls.

68. **Emerald Basin**

Trailhead: Follow Highway 1 to the Emerald Lake Road (2.6 km west of Field). Turn north (right), and follow the road 8 km to its end at the Emerald Lake parking lot. The trailhead is to the west (left) of the bridge.
Rating: harder, 4.3 km
Lighting: morning and afternoon

Emerald Basin is a glacial valley north of Emerald Lake, hemmed in by the summits of the President Range. The first 1.5 km of this trail utilizes the Emerald Lake lakeshore trail. The trail then turns left, crosses the alluvial fan, and turns left again into the trees. Af-ter a steep climb, the trail levels out in a pocket of old-growth forest of western red cedar and Douglas fir. Beyond the forest, the trail emerges into lush growth on the avalanche slope on the flanks of Emerald Peak. As the vegetation thins, the trail gradually becomes indistinct. Ahead is a hanging glacier, notched in the sheer limestone cliffs of The President and The Vice President.

69. **Deerlodge**

Trailhead: Follow Highway 1 for 22.6 km west of Field to the Hoodoo Creek Campground. Turn left and follow the campground road 600 m to a junction. Turn right on a gravel road, and follow this 400 m to the Deerlodge/Hoodoos trailhead. When the campground is closed (Sept. to June), you may have to park at the gate on the campground road, and walk to the trailhead.
Rating: easy, 0.5 km; 2.8 km loop if Nature Trail boardwalk is included
Lighting: anytime

Constructed in 1904, Deerlodge was the first warden patrol cabin in Yoho. Warden John Tocher and his wife May lived in the cabin from 1920 to 1926. At that time, the railway was the only connection to the outside world. Tocher brought the cookstove to the cabin by slinging it between two packhorses, and fording the Kicking Horse River.

The cabin was restored in 1961. The adjacent Nature Trail loops around a wetland. Use caution on the boardwalk, which was in disrepair at the time of publication. Beaver, moose, and great blue heron may be seen in the area.

KOOTENAY NATIONAL PARK

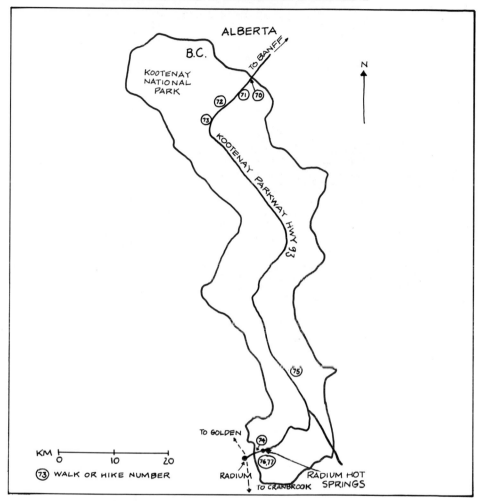

Kootenay National Park was established in 1920. British Columbia provided the necessary land, and in return the Canadian government constructed the Kootenay Parkway. This road, connecting Banff and the Columbia Valley, was the first highway completed across the Rockies. *Kootenay* is a native word meaning "people from beyond the hills."

Walks and easy hikes in Kootenay visit: a burnt forest, a dolomite canyon, an alpine valley glacier, and the outlets of three mineral springs. These trails are in excellent wildlife habitat. The Juniper Trail, in the southwestern corner of the park, introduces you to the drier, warmer climate of the Columbia Valley.

70. **Fireweed Trail**

Trailhead:
Kootenay Parkway
(Highway 93) at the
Continental Divide
(10.2 km west of
Castle Junction; 94.5
km east of the
junction with
Highway 95)
Rating: easy,
1 km loop
Lighting: anytime

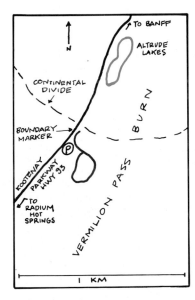

The Fireweed Trail loops through the Vermilion Pass Burn, providing a close-up view of the rebirth of a forest.

The summer of 1968 was hot and dry across most of western Canada. On the afternoon of July 8, the temperatures in Banff and Kootenay climbed to 30°C and winds were strong. At 4:30 p.m., a bolt of lightning struck the slopes of Mt. Whymper, just west of Vermilion Pass. Fanned by the winds, the lightning spark kindled a fire quickly. In three minutes, the mountainside was in flame. The

Vermilion Pass Burn had begun.

Despite the arrival of 65 fire-fighters within six hours, the forest fire burned out-of-control for three days. On July 12, the weather started to cool. The following day rain aided the firefighters, and by July 18 the fire was out. The Vermilion Pass burn consumed 2630 hectares (6500 acres) of subalpine forest, forced closure of the Kootenay Parkway, and cost $160,000 to fight. It sounds like a disaster, but this fire was part of a natural and essential process of succession – the regeneration of the forest.

Forest fires kill off diseased tree stands; reduce competition for moisture and sunlight; create stable seed beds by burning off loose soil layers; trigger the mass release of seeds; return minerals to the soil; and create habitat for wildlife.

The Vermilion Pass Burn consumed a mature forest of Engelmann spruce and subalpine fir, with scattered lodgepole pine. The resin-sealed cones of the lodgepoles were cracked open by the blaze, resulting in the mass seeding of a doghair forest.

By the year 2030, most of these lodgepole pines will be past their prime. Windfall and disease will take their toll, and the longer-lived Engelmann spruce and subalpine fir will then succeed the lodgepole pines to again become the dominant trees. If spruce and fir produce a second generation of trees before the next fire, the area will be described as a climax forest.

Studies of the Vermilion Pass Burn have yielded some interesting facts that illustrate the beneficial effect of forest fires. Within four years of the burn, there were nearly twice as many species of vegetation within the burned area as in the adjacent unburned area. The number of bird and other wildlife species using the burned area also increased.

On the negative side, avalanche terrain in Vermilion Pass has doubled since the burn.

Photo opposite: The blackened stumps and silver spars in Vermilion Pass are the remains of a subalpine forest that burned in 1968. The Fireweed Trail makes a short loop through the burn, where a new forest is growing from the remains of the old.

Common Fireweed

Among the silvery skeletons of the burned forest, common fireweed is sure to catch the eye. At home on disturbed ground, fireweed often grows in thickets. Each plant features many pink flowers, atop a stem that may reach two metres in height. The lowest flowers bloom first, and it is usual for flowers, buds, and purple seed pods all to be present on the same plant by late summer. The flowers shed a thick, yellow pollen. Common fireweed is the territorial emblem of the Yukon.

71. **Stanley Glacier**

Trailhead:
Kootenay Parkway
(Highway 93), 13.4
km west of Castle
Junction; 91.5 km
east of the junction
with Highway 95.
Rating: harder,
4.2 km
Lighting: anytime

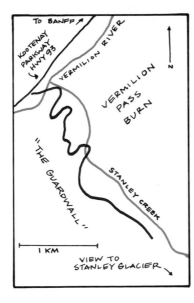

The Stanley Glacier trail leads into a spectacular glacial valley, and offers close up views of three major processes that have shaped the mountain environment: fire, avalanches, and glaciation. The trail is initially steep, gaining 220 m of elevation in the first 2.4 km.

Leaving the parking lot, the trail immediately crosses the Vermilion River and switchbacks up into the Vermilion Pass Burn. Most of the living trees at trailside are lodgepole pines that began to grow after the 1968 fire. After completing the climb, the trail descends slightly, to a footbridge that crosses Stanley Creek.

The next 1.8 km of trail is a hiker's delight. In the aftermath of the forest fire, with the shading canopy of trees removed, a variety of sun-loving wildflowers has invaded the area. Camas, fireweed, fleabane, pink wintergreen, arnica, yellow columbine, black-tipped groundsel, and vibrantly coloured Indian paintbrush are the most common species. Damp areas feature bog orchids and gentians.

At one point, the trail separates burned from unburned forest. On your right are mature Engelmann spruce; on the left are blackened timbers and stumps. You will not see as many young pines here as are near the trailhead. Growth in this part of the burn is progressing very slowly because cold air that drains from Stanley Glacier collects here, shortening the growing season.

The colossal 800 m high limestone cliff on the southwest side of the valley is known as The Guardwall. The dark streaks on the cliff are water seeps and lichen. In winter, the seeps freeze into sheets of ice and become a destination for waterfall ice climbers. The northeast wall of the valley features steep avalanche paths, swept annually by snowslides. At trailside are the sun-bleached remains of trees uprooted by the sliding snow and by the winds it generates.

A sign on a rocky knoll marks the end of the maintained trail. This is a good place to view Stanley Glacier. Several lobes of the glacier terminate at the cliff edge. You may hear the creaking and groaning of the ice as it creeps forward, and if fortunate witness an ice avalanche. Meltwater cascading over the cliffs is sometimes caught in updrafts, creating waterfalls that seem to disappear in midair.

The upper valley toward the glacier is a barren world of boulders and screes. It is home to mountain goat, hoary marmot, pika, and white-tailed ptarmigan. Stanley Peak was first climbed in 1901, by Edward Shymper of Matterhorn fame.

Photo opposite: The Stanley Glacier Trail leads through the Vermilion Pass Burn into a glacial side valley. Highlights of the trail include an array of wildflowers, an 800 m high limestone cliff, and views of Stanley Glacier.

U-Shaped Valley

The original valleys in the Rockies were V-shaped; products of erosion by water. When glacial ice advanced into these valleys, it undercut the adjoining mountainsides, causing them to collapse. The result was widened, U-shaped valleys known as troughs. You can see the U-shape in the view down-valley from the end of the Stanley Glacier trail.

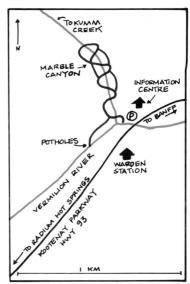

72. **Marble Canyon**

Photo above: The interpretive trail at Marble Canyon follows the canyon created by a retreating waterfall, and crosses Tokumm Creek seven times on sturdy bridges. The 600 m long canyon has a maximum depth of 39 m.

Trailhead: Kootenay Parkway (Highway 93); 17.2 km west of Castle Junction; 88 km east of the junction with Highway 95

Rating: easy, 800 m

Lighting: late morning and early afternoon

It has been said that in the Rockies, "the sound of rushing water is the sound of a canyon growing." To walk the Marble Canyon interpretive trail is to witness the truth in this statement. The trail follows the path of a "migrating" waterfall, the principal agent in creating Marble Canyon.

As with most canyons in the Rockies, Marble Canyon is at the mouth of a hanging valley, where Tokumm Creek joins the Vermilion River. (Tokumm is a native word meaning "red fox.") At the first bridge across Tokumm Creek, the hiker is greeted by a blast of cold air – a potent illustration of the canyon's effect on local climate. The temperature on the bridge can be 10°C colder than on the trail 20 metres away. Glaciers 20 km up the valley create a cold airflow, which is further cooled by the constant spray in the canyon and by the thermal mass of the shaded canyon walls. The spray saturates the canyon's edge, causing soils to creep towards the abyss. Only mosses, lichens, and plants with mat-like characteristics can anchor these soils and grow here.

The trail crosses the canyon seven times on sturdy bridges. A natural arch – a lip of rock which resisted erosion – can be seen from the second bridge. This arch marks the waterfall's location, 9000 years ago. Please don't attempt to cross it. People have died from falls at this very spot.

The large sedimentary boulder near the fifth bridge is a glacial erratic, deposited here when the glacier receded. Cracks in its surface have filled with soil, and a tree has taken root. The canyon's gradual, leftward curve resulted from the water enlarging a crack system in the underlying bedrock. Marble Canyon's deepest point is the 39 m drop beneath the seventh bridge, the present location of the waterfall.

The main rock types in Marble Canyon are limestone and the more resistant dolomite. Dolomite will naturally become the lip of the waterfall in this canyon, resisting the water's flow while the surrounding limestone is more easily eroded. The constant pounding at the base of the waterfall creates a plunge pool, which enlarges over time and begins to undercut the lip of the waterfall above. Eventually, gravity, the shattering effects of frost,

and the sheer hydraulic force of the water will prevail. The hanging dolomite lip of the waterfall will collapse into the plunge pool, and the brink will move a few metres upstream. In this manner the waterfall has migrated more than 600 m upstream in Marble Canyon, in 11,000 years.

Is It Marble?

Some people consider Marble Canyon a misnomer, claiming there is no marble in the canyon. By strict geological definition, this is correct. True marble is limestone or dolomite where the carbonates have been recrystallized by heat or pressure. However, in common usage, marble refers to limey sedimentary rock that can be polished. The 540-million-year-old Cathedral dolomite in Marble Canyon is polished constantly by glacial silt in the water, and yields a fine finish. So a layman would call it marble. The best "marble" is the whitish coloured rock at the brink of the waterfall.

Slightly downstream from Marble Canyon are potholes eroded into another exposure of highly polished dolomite. They may be reached on your return by taking the branch trail to the right, just before recrossing the first bridge.

73. **Ochre Beds and Paint Pots**

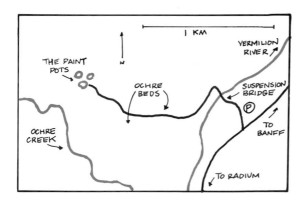

Trailhead:
Kootenay Parkway
(Highway 93), 19.7
km west of Castle
Junction; 85 km east

of the junction with
Highway 95
Rating: easy, 1 km
Lighting: anytime

The walk to the Ochre Beds and Paint Pots leads to colourful deposits of clay and to the outlets of three mineral springs. On the way, you are treated to a crossing of the Vermilion River by suspension bridge. Wildlife is common in the vicinity of the Ochre Beds. Look for: wolf, coyote, deer, elk, moose, American marten, grizzly bear, and black bear. You may see their tracks in the clay.

The clay at the Ochre Beds was created from sediments deposited on the bottom of an ancient glacial lake. The remarkable colours result from saturation of the clay with iron-rich water. This water emerges at the three mineral springs – The Paint Pots. The iron compounds in the water have also stained rocks and vegetation in the Vermilion River, providing its name.

The Ochre Beds were known to Kootenay Natives from the interior of B.C. as "the place where the red earth spirit is taken." The Kootenays gathered the colourful clay, formed it into cakes, and baked it in fire. The resulting compound was ground into powder and mixed with animal fat or fish grease to create a body paint, used in rituals.

The Kootenays discovered that the "red earth" was a valuable trading commodity. Once or twice a year, they would cross the Rockies to hunt bison and trade with the Stoneys at Kootenay Plains on the North Saskatchewan River. One of their trade and travel routes, known as the Kootenay Trail, went northwest from the Ochre Beds. Ochre and bison bones have been found at many archeological sites along the Kootenay Trail in Yoho and Banff national parks.

In the early 1900s, commercial interests developed the Ochre Beds as a source of pigment for paint. The clay was excavated and hauled overland to Castle Junction and shipped to Calgary by train. The enterprise soon failed. Equipment remains at the Ochre Beds, rusting beside mounds of clay heaped up for a harvest that was never completed.

Visitors today are requested not to walk in the ochre deposits, or remove any of the material. The clay will stain clothing and shoes, and disturbances of this soil take many years to disappear.

Photo opposite: The Paint Pots are the three mineral springs that provide the red and yellow stains in The Ochre Beds.

The Paint Pots

The Paint Pots are cone-shaped mineral spring outlets, with water emerging at a relatively cool temperature of 10.7°C. Either the water does not seep far enough underground to become super-heated, or it becomes intermixed with cold water on its return to the surface. The volume of flow is 330 litres per minute.

The cones around the Paint Pots build up through an accumulation of iron oxide, precipitated from the spring water as it emerges from the ground. As the iron oxide rim grows in height, the pool gets deeper. The deeper water creates a back pressure greater than the pressure of the flowing spring water. The spring is then forced to seek another outlet where the resistance is less, leaving behind an abandoned or "choked" cone. There are several choked cones in the vicinity of the Paint Pots.

The two largest Paint Pots contain a mixture of spring and surface water, and are greenish in colour. The water of the smallest Paint Pot is pure and clear. Sedges, cotton grass, and tall white bog orchids grow in the moist area nearby.

74. **Juniper Trail**

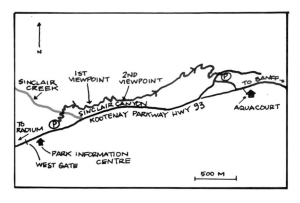

The Juniper Trail descends from the Kootenay Parkway to Sinclair Creek, and then climbs to viewpoints on the rim of Sinclair Canyon. Bighorn sheep are often seen on this hike.

Trailhead: Kootenay Parkway (Highway 93) 200 m from the Kootenay National Park gate; (103.5 km west of Castle Junction; 1.2 km east of the junction with Highway 95). **Rating**: harder, 4.6 km loop **Lighting**: anytime

The Juniper Trail is the most "up and down" outing in this book. The trail initially takes an abrupt descent to Sinclair Creek, followed by a steady climb to the rim of the canyon above. The rewards for hiking this steep trail are spectacular views over the Columbia Valley and an appreciation of the diverse vegetation in the area of Radium Hot Springs.

From the parking area 200 m north of the park gate, the trail switchbacks steeply down to Sinclair Creek. During the descent, you will notice changes in the vegetation, produced by the damp, cool canyon air. Mosses appear on the trunks of Douglas firs, and feather mosses carpet the forest floor in the shade of western red cedars. Before crossing the creek on the bridge, walk upstream a short distance on a rough trail for a view of the waterfall at the mouth of Sinclair Canyon.

After crossing Sinclair Creek, the trail begins its climb to the rim of Sinclair Canyon. If you pay attention to the surrounding vegetation, you will notice another pronounced change at the first switchback. The cedars and feather mosses disappear, replaced by widely spaced Douglas fir, grasses, bearberry, and juniper. This vegetation is typical of the adjacent Columbia Valley, which features a milder, drier climate than the Rockies. Because of their steepness and sunny aspect, slopes like this one remain virtually snow-free all winter. They provide important habitat for bighorn sheep.

From the second and highest viewpoint, there is a fine view west to Mt. Farnham, in the Purcell Range of the Columbia Mountains. Wetlands further north in the Columbia Valley are also visible. These are important stopovers and nesting areas for migratory birds.

The short descent north delivers the hiker to a parking area near the Aquacourt and the colourful cliffs of the Redwall. If a dip in the hot springs is not in your itinerary, follow the sidewalk to your right, 1.4 kilometres back to the trailhead.

The Columbia Valley, into which Sinclair Creek empties, occupies a tremendous rift in the earth's surface. Known as the Rocky Mountain Trench, this rift parallels the entire western boundary of the Rockies, separating them from the older Columbia Mountains.

Before construction of hydroelectric dams on the Columbia River, chinook salmon could migrate from the Pacific back along the river to spawn at its headwaters. However, the dams have proved insurmountable, and attempts to re-establish the salmon run have failed. The annual migration is now curtailed 600 km downriver from here. Salmon are an important source of food for both animals and Native people. The disappearance of the salmon has greatly affected the ecology of the Columbia Valley.

Juniper

Juniper is an evergreen cypress shrub, with three species that grow in the Rockies. Prickly juniper grows in circular patches. Creeping juniper grows from a trailing vine. And the Rocky Mountain juniper is a shrub that may reach 5 m in height. Both the creeping and Rocky Mountain juniper have shreddy bark and scaly leaves, like their enormous cypress cousin, the western red cedar.

Prickly juniper is the most common of the three types, and is aptly named. Contact with the spiky needles produces a rash in some people. All junipers grow berries, which vary in colour from green to grey to purple, depending on age. The berries may stay on the plant for two summers, and provide food for birds and squirrels. In days past, they were used to flavour gin. The photograph shows a branch of the Rocky Mountain juniper.

OTHER WALKS AND HIKES IN KOOTENAY NATIONAL PARK

See map on page 115

75. Dog Lake

Trailhead: Kootenay Parkway (Highway 93; 78 km west of Castle Junction; 27 km east of the junction with Highway 95), 500 m west of McLeod Meadows Campground
Rating: moderate, 2.6 km
Lighting: anytime

Dog Lake makes an ideal excursion for campers staying at McLeod Meadows Campground. From the picnic area, the trail skirts the rear of the campground and crosses the Kootenay River on two bridges. It then climbs east away from the river through a Douglas fir forest. Western wood lilies bloom here in early summer. After you walk over a low ridge, the sounds of the highway disappear, and the trail drops toward peaceful Dog Lake. The lake's outlet shows evidence of a beaver dam. By crossing a footbridge, it is possible to follow a rough and wet track (used by fishermen) to the lake's east shore. Many of the lodgepole pines in this part of the Kootenay Valley have been afflicted by mountain pine beetle – hence the discoloured foliage.

76. Valleyview

Trailhead: Junction of highway 93 and 95; 500 m south of the junction take the Redstreak Campground Road. The trailhead is 200 m west of the entrance to Redstreak Campground, on the left.
Rating: moderate, 1.2 km
Lighting: anytime

The Valleyview Trail traverses steep, grassy slopes which support an open Douglas fir forest, to a viewpoint overlooking the Columbia Valley. Red squirrel, pileated woodpecker, and ruffed grouse inhabit this forest, and in late spring and early summer, a variety of wildflowers blooms on the sunny slopes. The last 300 m of trail is a staircase which descends to Radium Hot Springs townsite.

77. Redstreak

Trailheads: To hike downhill: follow the Redstreak Campground Road to the trailhead at Loop H. To hike uphill: begin at the rear of the Aquacourt on Highway 93.
Rating: moderate, 2.3 km
Lighting: anytime

The Redstreak Trail is recommended to campers who wish to visit the Aquacourt and obtain a spectacular view into Sinclair Canyon on the way. The side trail to the Sinclair Canyon Viewpoint is reached in 300 m from the campground. Look for bighorn sheep on the steep, grassy slopes on the opposite side of the canyon. Back on the Redstreak Trail, you drop steadily to the Aquacourt, and the forest becomes increasingly damp and dense. The young trees immediately above the Aquacourt grew after a 1967 forest fire.

WATERTON LAKES NATIONAL PARK

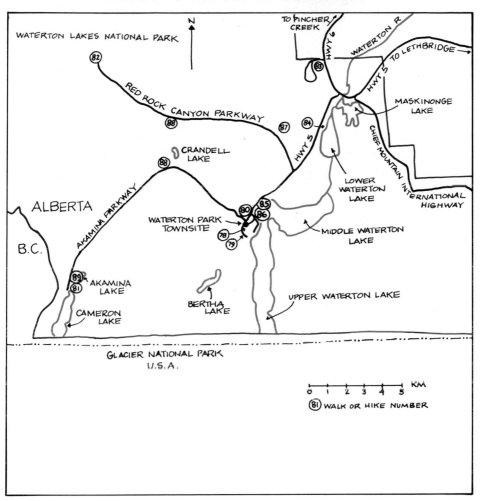

W aterton Lakes National Park is located where the mountains meet the prairie. This, the smallest of the Rocky Mountain parks features: vistas of this unique landscape, human history, interesting geology, and diverse plant and animal life. More than one half of Alberta's plant species are found in Waterton. The wildflower displays of late spring and early summer are among the best in the Canadian Rockies.

The Waterton Lakes provide opportunity for fishing and water sports. Many visitors to the park come prepared to take part in these activities.

78. **Cameron Falls and Waterton Townsite**

Trailhead: Cameron Falls. Follow Cameron Falls Drive or Evergreen Avenue to the parking lot at the bridge over Cameron Creek.
Rating: easy, 3.2 km loop. Wheelchair accessible
Lighting: anytime; Cameron Falls best in the morning

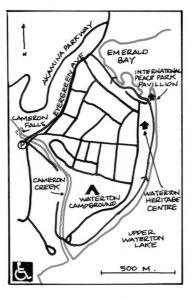

The circuit of Waterton townsite is an ideal introduction to Waterton Lakes, established in 1911 as Canada's fifth national park. Cameron Falls makes a logical starting point for this walk, which is mostly on a brick sidewalk.

Cameron Falls cascades over a 10 m high limestone step. This limestone is the 1.5 billion year old Waterton Formation – the oldest rock visible in the Canadian Rockies. A short trail on the right of the waterfall offers access to the rim of the canyon which has been cut by Cameron Creek.

From Cameron Falls, cross the road and follow the path downstream along Cameron Creek towards Upper Waterton Lake. The creek bed shows evidence of shoring and man-made diversions, designed to mitigate the effects of flash floods. Waterton townsite is also susceptible to flooding from high waters on the lake. The most recent serious flooding was in 1975.

If the day is typical at Waterton, it will be windy. The average daily wind speed is 32.5 km per hour at the townsite. Chinook winds, which can raise the temperature 40°C in a few hours, contribute to the warmest winters in Alberta. However, the park also has the highest annual precipitation in the province and the greatest annual snowfall in Canada east of the Continental Divide.

Turn northward (left) at the lakeshore, and follow the sidewalk towards town. You can make a visit to the Waterton Heritage Centre, where exhibits describe the history of the park. A few hundred metres farther is the International Peace Park Pavilion, constructed in 1982 for the 50th anniversary of the Waterton-Glacier International Peace Park. The peace park, an expression of goodwill between Canada and the United States, was the first of its kind in the world.

The marine vessel, *The International* departs from the nearby marina on Emerald Bay, touring Upper Waterton Lake into U.S. waters. The maiden voyage of *The*

International was in 1927, the year the Prince of Wales Hotel opened. At the bottom of Emerald Bay lies a paddle wheel steamship, brought to Waterton in 1907 to tow log booms. Later it was moored at the dock and used as a tearoom. It was scuttled in 1918. Today, the novelty of a shipwreck in inland waters attracts divers from throughout western Canada.

After passing the marina, turn south (left) on Evergreen Avenue to return to the Cameron Falls parking lot, or turn north (right) to reach the Prince of Wales and Linnet Lake trails.

Photo opposite:
Cameron Falls is one of the highlights of the walk around Waterton townsite. The rock beneath the falls is limestone, 1.5 billion year old – the oldest rock visible in the Rockies.

The Oldest Rock in the Rockies

How did 1.5-billion-year-old limestone from the sedimentary basement of the Rockies, come to rest on the surface? The sediment, particles of mud, sand, and pebbles, that became the rocks in the Rockies, were deposited on the floors of ancient seas in horizontal layers. During mountain building, which lasted from approximately 120 to 60 million years ago, compressive forces pushed these sedimentary formations northeast. Within the earth's crust, higher temperatures made the rock pliable. Under the pressure, the rock bowed into folds. Some of these folds broke, and massive sheets of rock were freed to slide as thrust sheets, riding upwards and over adjacent rock to the northeast. In this manner, rocks from deep within the earth's crust were brought toward the surface. Since then, these ancient rocks have been exposed through the erosion of overlying rock layers.

79. **Lower Bertha Falls**

Photo above: The Bertha Falls Trail explores the montane forest south of Waterton townsite. It leads to a viewpoint overlooking Upper Waterton Lake, and then follows the Bertha Valley to a picturesque waterfall.

Trailhead: Evergreen Avenue, 500 m south of Cameron Falls
Rating: moderate, 2.9 km. Brochure available at park information centre
Lighting: morning

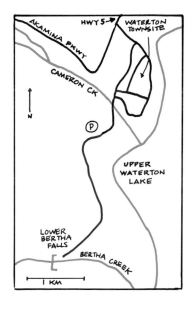

The hike to Lower Bertha Falls explores the montane forest and delivers the hiker to a picturesque waterfall – a cool, shady destination on a hot day. Pick up a brochure at the park information centre for a detailed explanation of the eight stops en route. Keep right at all trail junctions.

A glance through the brochure reveals: avalanches, blowdowns, beetle infestations, and forest fires. It sounds like a rollcall of destruction. Though many of the transformations in this forest are subtle, nature often resorts to destruction to make beneficial changes. The blowdown on the Bertha Falls trail took place June 7, 1964, when wind speeds reached more than 160 km per hour. In all, 200 hectares (500 acres) of the park were affected that day. Blowdowns remove weakened trees and create new habitat for wildlife by opening up the forest.

At Km 1.7 the trail emerges from the trees to reveal a wonderful panorama of Upper Waterton Lake and the mountains along its east shore, the highest is Mt. Cleveland, in Montana. Limber pine, a rare tree in the Rockies, grows in the vicinity of this viewpoint. Leaving the viewpoint, the trail swings to the southwest (right), climbing gradually into the Bertha Lake valley.

Lower Bertha Falls is reached in another kilometre. Water cascades in a veil across a tilted, resistant outcrop of rock. At the base of the falls, the stream has been captured by the edge of another resistant rock formation, producing a right-angle turn in the direction of flow.

High annual precipitation and shade near the falls allow several plant species to grow that are normally associated with coastal forests. "Bertha" was Bertha Ekelund, an early Waterton resident who was jailed for passing counterfeit money.

Mountain Pine Beetle

The mountain pine beetle infests over-mature pine trees. The female beetle bores through the tree bark and deposits her eggs in the soft layer beneath. The worm-like burrowings that the female and her offspring chew beneath the bark, girdle the tree and kill it by drying up the sap flow. Examples of these burrowings are visible on dead pines beside the Lower Bertha Falls trail.

The most recent beetle infestation in Waterton ran its course between 1976 and 1983. More than half the pines in the park were killed. Some stands were totally destroyed. The severity was so great because Waterton's forests are over-mature.

For the past 50 years, all forest fires have been suppressed in the park. Without the rejuvenating process of fire, nature has resorted to using the pine beetle, in an attempt to regenerate the forest.

The death of the pines has exposed a greater area of the forest floor to sunlight, resulting in new growth needed by wildlife. Removal of the pines has also made way for succession to a forest dominated by spruce and Douglas fir, the climax species for this area. One objective of national park policy is to ensure the continuation of natural processes. Although this forest looks devastated; it is not. A natural transformation is taking place that will ultimately benefit all the species that live here.

80. **Bear's Hump**

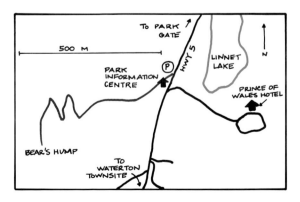

Upper Waterton Lake and Waterton townsite from the Bear's Hump. Hikers earn this spectacular view, since the trail gains more than 200 vertical metres in only 1.2 km.

Trailhead: Waterton Park Information Centre, 1 km north of the townsite on Highway 5.
Rating: harder, 1.2 km
Lighting: anytime

The Bear's Hump is a limestone bluff on a ridge of Mt. Crandell. The trail to its crest is the second steepest in this book. The hiker's reward for completing this unrelenting climb is a panorama that includes: Waterton Lakes, Waterton Townsite, and the contact between mountain and prairie that makes the park famous. Waterton is a windy park, and the Bear's Hump is one of its windiest places. Take a sweater and windbreaker with you. Avoid this hike when there are thunderstorms nearby.

From the summit of the Bear's Hump, Upper Waterton Lake is the centrepiece in the view. The lake has an area of 941 hectares (2324 acres), is 11.1 km long, and is 750 m wide. It extends 4 km into Montana. It holds aapproximately 645 million cubic metres of water. At a maximum depth of 157 m, it is the deepest lake in the Canadian Rockies.

The Upper Waterton Valley was created by a glacier that undercut the adjacent mountainsides. The resulting U-shaped trough is quite visible. The glacier also eroded the hollow in the bedrock that is now the lake bed. The Middle and Lower Waterton

Lakes formed in a different manner. They are kettle ponds, created by the melting of detached blocks of glacial ice.

From the summit of the Bear's Hump you can also see Waterton townsite. It is built on an alluvial fan. Boulders, silt, and rubble are borne away from mountains in streams and rivers, and deposited when the angle of the stream bed lessens, creating an alluvial fan. This fan has formed where Cameron Creek drops from its hanging valley into the Waterton Valley. It is thought much of the material in alluvial fans in the Rockies was deposited during a tremendous meltwater surge between 6000 and 7000 years ago. Material is still being deposited on the Waterton fan today, although diversions of Cameron Creek (designed to prevent flooding) have interfered with the natural process.

Looking north from the Bear's Hump, the front ranges of the Rockies end abruptly on the prairie. During mountain building approximately 85 million years ago, the rock formations which make up Waterton's mountains were thrust northeastwards as a cohesive, 6.5 km thick mass of rock, known as the Lewis Thrust Sheet. This huge slab of rock slid 60 to 70 km, and came to rest atop undisturbed, relatively flat shales. The mountains were literally pushed onto the prairie, and the effect is still visible today.

A Natural Dam, A Man-made Dam

The streamlined contours of the Bear's Hump indicate it was completely covered by glacial ice during the Wisconsin Glaciation. Before that ice age, the Bear's Hump was connected to Vimy Peak on the opposite side of the lakes. The Bosporus, the narrow channel joining Upper and Middle Waterton lakes, was eroded through this connecting ridge by the ancestral Waterton Glacier. Evidence of the connecting ridge can be seen in the knoll beneath the Prince of Wales Hotel, and the rocky spur known as "the couch" that extends to waterline on the opposite side of the Bosporus.

Glaciers removed this natural rock dam. In 1919, a proposal was made to construct a concrete dam at the Bosporus, to impound Upper Waterton Lake for irrigation. A dam would have greatly altered the ecology and the appeal of the national park. Fortunately, the proposal was dismissed by James B. Harkin, Commissioner of Dominion Parks.

81. **Cameron Lake**

Cameron Lake is located in a glacially carved valley in the extreme southwest corner of Alberta. Mt. Custer, at the far end of the lake, lies entirely within Glacier National Park, Montana.

Trailhead: Follow the Akamina Parkway for 16 km from Waterton townsite to the end of the road, at the Cameron Lake parking lot.
Rating: easy, 1.6 km
Lighting: morning and late afternoon

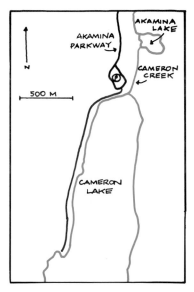

The Cameron Lake trail takes you into the extreme southwest corner of Alberta – a place where two parks, two provinces, and two countries meet. The trail south along the west side of the lake is through pleasant subalpine forest. The trail is flat, making it ideal for family walks. The lake is also popular with fishermen.

Although glaciers have long been absent from Waterton's mountains, their legacy is evident at Cameron Lake. The lake is situated in a bowl-shaped valley known as a cirque. A glacier that once occupied the flanks of Mt. Custer at the far end of the lake eroded the cirque. The glacier also flowed northward, creating the lake's hollow and depositing the moraine that now dams the lake.

The common trees in the subalpine forest around Cameron Lake are Engelmann spruce and subalpine fir, both coniferous. There are many ways of telling coniferous tree species apart, but to the casual visitor with an interest in botany, needles provide the easiest clue. Fir needles are flat, spruce needles are spikey and square, and lodgepole pine needles occur in pairs. If the needles are spikey to touch, you have a spruce; likewise, if a needle will roll between your fingers. If the needles are flat and will not roll between your fingers, you have a subalpine or Douglas fir. If the needles are in bundles of two, you have a lodgepole pine; if in bundles of five, the less common whitebark pine or the limber pine. (Please be gentle with tree branches and needles, and do not trample vegetation.)

The subalpine forest is often called the "snow forest" – a name that is most appropriate at Cameron Lake. Nearby Akamina (ah-kah-MEE-nuh) Pass records the highest annual snowfall in Alberta. The spire-like form of the subalpine fir helps shed the heavy snow load.

The undergrowth at trailside around Cameron Lake features: Arnica, queen's cup, cow parsnip, foam flower, dwarf dogwood,

purple geranium, false hellebore, pearly everlasting, and the attractive red monkey flower. The red monkey flower is a favourite with both hummingbirds and amateur botanists. The only other national park in the Rockies where this flower is found is Jasper.

Avalanche Paths

Snow avalanches are one of the most common and important natural processes in the Rockies. Accumulations of snow will slide as a mass down a mountainside depending on the kind of slope and the weather and snow conditions. The force of the avalanche and the wind blast it generates, creates a swath in the forest. Supple willows and alders will survive by bending. Mat-like plants, grasses, and wildflowers survive by flattening beneath the snow.

Avalanches create openings in the forest, allowing sunlight to reach the ground. These openings promote a growth of vegetation for elk, deer, moose, and bears. The avalanche paths at the end of the Cameron Lake trail are frequented by grizzly bears. They feed on the lush growth of plants such as cow parsnip

82. **Red Rock Canyon**

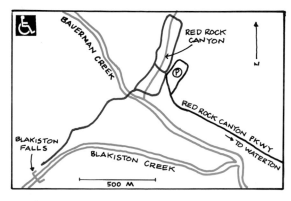

Trailhead: From the junction of Highway 5 and the Red Rock Canyon Parkway, drive along the parkway to the end of the road – the parking lot at Red Rock Canyon.

Rating: easy, 700 m loop. Wheelchair accessible

Lighting: anytime

The paved trail at Red Rock Canyon makes a circuit of one of the most colourful attractions in the Rockies. The red rock in the canyon is a 1.5 billion year old mudstone, known as argillite (ARE-jill-ite). This rock was formed from iron-rich sediments deposited on ancient tidal mud flats. Where the mud flats were exposed to air, the iron oxidized and turned red. The green and white rocks in the canyon are also argillite, but contain iron that did not oxidize.

Red Rock Canyon is 23 m deep, and began forming 10,000 years ago. Its steep walls indicate rapid erosion. The potholes were created by swirling rocks trapped in eddies. The Canyon also has some uncommon features. These include ripple rock that records wave action along a prehistoric shoreline. On the east side of the canyon, the trail crosses a honeycomb of mud cracks. These cracks opened when mud dried on an ancient tidal flat. The cracks were later filled with a different type of sediment. The formation was subsequently turned to rock by the pressure of other sediments that accumulated above.

At trailside are examples of a fossil known as a stromatolite. These reef-like accumulations were created 1.5 billion years ago, from calcium carbonate produced by algae. Similar algae grow today, creating reefs in warm, shallow seas.

The last item of geological interest is an intrusion of igneous (once molten) rock, near the mouth of the canyon. Nearly all rock in the Rockies was sedimentary in origin. However, blobs of molten rock sometimes found their way into cracks within the hardened sedimentary layers or onto the earth's surface. The dark grey igneous rock here, is a lava known as basalt (BAH-salt.)

A native travel route known as The Buffalo Trail, crossed South Kootenay Pass and followed Blakiston Creek past the mouth of Red Rock Canyon. Seasonal native hunting camps have been found near the canyon, and are dated to 8000 years ago.

You may extend this outing by walking a kilometre southwest from the mouth of Red Rock Canyon to the viewing platform at Blakiston Falls. The falls were named for Lt. Thomas Blakiston, meteorologist with the Palliser Expedition of 1857-60. Blakiston was the first recorded European visitor to what is now Waterton Lakes National Park. He travelled along Blakiston Creek in 1858.

Photo opposite: The red, white, and green mudstones of Red Rock Canyon are 1.5 billion years old, one of the oldest rock formations visible in the Rockies. The canyon presents an opportunity to see bighorn sheep, fossils, and intriguing geology.

Too Many Feet

The Red Rock Canyon Parkway was completed in the 1920s. Since then, millions of people have visited the canyon, and the effect of millions of pairs of feet on the mudstone is very noticeable. Though erosion of the rock by water is a natural phenomenon, excessive erosion resulting from foot traffic is not. By all means, appreciate the canyon. But please, keep to the paved walkway and bridges, and spare the 1.5 billion year old mudstone from further damage.

The band of bighorn sheep which frequents Red Rock Canyon has also suffered from interaction with humans. These animals are so accustomed to handouts, they now expect to be fed by everyone. Please refrain. It endangers both sheep and humans

83. **Bison Paddock Viewpoint**

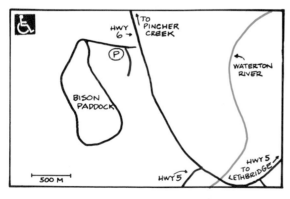

Trailhead: Follow Highway 6 north, for 2 km from its junction with   Highway 5 to the Bison Paddock Road. Turn left and park on the left.   **Rating**: easy, 300 m. Wheelchair accessible

Lighting: morning

There is no finer place to appreciate Waterton's mountain/prairie contact than the Bison Paddock Viewpoint. Here, the rolling shortgrass prairie, dotted with kettle lakes, stops abruptly at the base of Bellevue Hill and the front ranges of the Rockies. The grasses and wildflowers of the bison paddock prairie represent the natural vegetation of the northern interior plains. There are very few pockets of this kind of vegetation left, and that is part of the tale of the bison's demise.

As many as 60 million bison lived on the interior plains in 1790. When horses and rifles were introduced, the bison was subjected to a senseless slaughter. The prairie was also burned off and put under the plow as settlers arrived. Diseases imported with domestic cattle also took a heavy toll on the bison. What was the net result of all this pressure? By 1890, the population of the plains bison was 1090. The decimation of this animal was a double tragedy, unparalleled in history, for it also spelled the end of the traditional native way of life.

The revival of the plains bison from near extinction can be attributed to Walking Coyote, a man who captured bison in southern Alberta in 1874 and sold them to two ranchers in Montana. In 1907, the Canadian government purchased 716 bison from the captive Montana herd. Descendants of these bison now make up the exhibition herds at various national parks, including Waterton Lakes. The Waterton Lakes bison paddock was established in 1952, with one bull and five cows. Today, approximately two dozen bison live here.

The bison paddock area features many glacial landforms. The lakes are kettle ponds. The sinuous gravel ridges are eskers, which were deposited in streams running beneath glacial ice. Other mounds are drumlins – oval-shaped heaps of rubble left behind by the ice; and kames – conical shaped piles of rubble de-

posited at a glacier's edge by meltwater flowing from the glacier's surface. The viewpoint is on a kame.

There are also many archaeological sites in this vicinity. A nearby cliff was used as a bision jump.

Photo opposite: Waterton's famous mountain/prairie contact is the highlight in this view from the Bison Paddock Viewpoint.

Bison

The bison (BYE-sun) is the largest land mammal in North America. The popular name, "buffalo," is more correctly applied to certain wild cattle of Asia and Africa. Adult male bison stand 1.7 m tall at the shoulder, and weigh 725 to 1000 kg. There are two species: plains and wood. The bison in the Waterton Lakes Bison Paddock are plains bison. Those at Banff are the slightly larger wood bison.

Bison watchers will notice the animals like to wallow in dirt and dust. The dirt reduces irritation from insects and shedding skin. It is not uncommon for bison to allow birds on their backs. A bird brings relief to the bison by eating insects from the bison's coat.

Bison have a heavy and clumsy appearance that belies their agility and speed. They can sprint 60 km per hour. They are quite territorial and defensive and readily show aggression to tourists. If you drive through one of the national park bison paddocks, please remain in your vehicle. Bison can be long-lived; one of the original bison at Banff was 38 when he died.

OTHER WALKS AND HIKES IN WATERTON LAKES NATIONAL PARK

See map on page 127

84. Kootenai Brown's Grave

Trailhead: Highway 5, 3 km south of its junction with Highway 6; 5.4 km north of Waterton townsite
Rating: easy, 500 m
Lighting: anytime

This trail visits the grave of John Kootenai Brown, who was in many ways the father of Waterton Lakes National Park. A character who epitomized the "wild west," Brown's pre-Waterton life read like an encyclopedia of adventure. He served with the British Army in India, made and lost a fortune in the Cariboo gold fields, served as a police constable at Cranbrook, rode as a pony express rider, trapped for furs, ran whiskey, and was accused and acquitted of murdering a business partner. Brown first saw the Waterton Lakes in 1865, and he returned three years later to settle near the mouth of Blakiston Creek.

The idyllic life Brown enjoyed, guiding and trapping at Waterton, was disrupted in the 1890s. He had witnessed the demise of the plains bison, and now increasing numbers of visitors were threatening other wildlife and fish populations. Together with local ranchers, Brown pressured the federal government to set aside a reserve in the area, and in 1895 the Kootenay Lakes Forest Reserve was established. (The Waterton Lakes had been originally known as the Kootenay Lakes.) Brown became the first guardian of the protected area.

In 1911, the reserve was proclaimed a national park, and its name changed to Waterton Lakes. At age 71, Brown became the park's first superintendent; a position he held for three years. The park area was then increased thirty-fold, requiring a younger man in the patrol saddle. Brown died in 1916. He is buried on the shore of Lower Waterton Lake between the graves of his two wives.

85. Linnet Lake

Trailhead: Drive 400 m north of the Park Information Centre on Highway 5. The parking and picnic area is across from the government compound
Rating: easy, 1 km paved loop. Wheelchair accessible
Lighting: anytime

The Linnet Lake trail was paved in 1985 as a park project to commemorate the national parks centennial. The lake is a kettle pond. The surrounding forest features Douglas fir, balsam poplar, white birch, lodgepole pine, and the shrub, saskatoon. A linnet is a type of finch.

86. Prince of Wales

Trailheads: Highway 5, 400 m north of the park information centre. Or use the Emerald Bay picnic area, 300 m south of the Park Information Centre.
Rating: moderate, 2 km loop
Lighting: anytime

The Prince of Wales Hotel was the brainchild of Louis Hill, president of the Great Northern Railway.

With Glacier National Park established as a major tourist draw in the U.S., Hill sought to expand his business into Canada. Construction of the hotel began in in 1926 and proceeded not without incident. Chinook winds, gusting to 144 km per hour, pushed the hotel 20 cm off its foundation. However the hotel opened the following summer and soon became a successful industry as well as part of Waterton's trademark view.

The hotel sits on top of a glacial deposit known as a kame – a conical pile of boulders and sediments deposited at the edge of a retreating glacier, by meltwater flowing from the surface of the ice. This kame is especially high because it accumulated on a bedrock bench that formerly connected Mt. Crandell (west of Upper Waterton Lake) with Vimy Peak to the east.

The trail loops around the base of the kame, crossing a pebbled beach to the narrows of The Bosporus. The Bosporus separates Upper and Middle Waterton lakes and is a favourite fishing spot. The stunted and gnarled shapes of trees are evidence of Waterton's windiness. After following the lakeshore north to the Linnet Lake trailhead, the Prince of Wales Trail climbs back over the kame, and descends to the picnic area at Emerald Bay.

87. **Bellevue Prairie**

Trailhead: Follow the Red Rock Canyon Parkway, 2.9 km from Highway 5, to where the road makes a prominent left-hand turn. Park on the right. The trail is unsigned, and heads north from the road.

Rating: easy, 1-2 km

Lighting: morning

To walk the Bellevue Prairie is to explore the place where mountain and prairie meet. Although Waterton's peaks are not high by Rockies' standards, the abrupt manner in which they rise from the rolling prairie, makes this one of the most unique settings for a walk in the mountain national parks.

Waterton is extraordinarily rich in plant life. The park contains more than half of the plant species found in Alberta – 870 vascular plants, 182 mosses and liverworts, and 218 lichens. The Bellevue Prairie is a remnant of the shortgrass prairie which originally covered much of central North America. The plant associations found here occur nowhere else in the mountain national parks. The wildflowers are spectacular, and the walk is highly recommended to the amateur botanist, particularly in late spring and early summer.

The Bellevue Prairie is known to glaciologists as an eskerine complex. An esker is a sinuous ridge of gravelly material, deposited by meltwater flowing beneath a glacier. Many eskers snake their way across this prairie. Their windward sides lack trees, but in the shade and shelter of these low ridges, stunted aspens and limber pines grow.

The Buffalo Trail, an ancient native travel route between British Columbia and the plains of Alberta, crossed Bellevue Prairie. Archeological remains have been found in the area, including: rock structures associated with ritual sites, buffalo jumps, campsites, and the ruts left by native sleds.

While it is possible to walk across Bellevue Prairie to Indian Springs near the Bison Paddock, most walkers venture a kilometre or two out onto the prairie, and then backtrack to the Red Rock Canyon Parkway. Please keep to the trail to spare the vegetation.

88. **Crandell Lake**

Trailheads: Follow the Akamina Parkway, 6.6 km from Waterton townsite. Park on the right. Or, follow the Red Rock Canyon Parkway, 6 km from its junction with Highway 5. Turn south (left) onto the Canyon Camp Road (1.2 km past Crandell Campground) and follow it 400 m to the parking lot.
Ratings: From Akamina Parkway, easy, 1.6 km. From Red Rock Canyon Parkway, moderate, 2.4 km
Lighting: anytime

Crandell Lake is situated on a low bench separating the Cameron and Blakiston valleys. During the Wisconsin Glaciation, glacial ice flowed from the south over this bench, and scooped out the hollow that now contains the lake. Both trails to the lake are pleasant, and follow the route of an old wagon road that was constructed in 1902, to allow access to nearby oil wells. E.H. Crandell was a Calgary businessman who helped finance the Discovery Oil Well. The trails feature wildflowers, and there is a sandy beach amid a poplar grove at the lake's north end.

89. **Akamina Lake**

Trailhead: Follow the Akamina Parkway, 16 km from Waterton townsite to the Cameron Lake parking lot. The trail is on the east side of the parking lot.
Rating: easy, 500 m
Lighting: anytime

Akamina Lake is a peaceful body of water, a short walk from the hubbub of the Cameron Lake parking lot. The trail winds through wet subalpine forest to a platform on the lakeshore. There is opportunity to see moose, waterfowl, and fish. Horsetail, ferns, arnica, and foam flower are some of the common plants in the undergrowth. *Akamina* (ah-kah-MEE-nuh) is a native word that means "bench land."

MT. ROBSON PROVINCIAL PARK

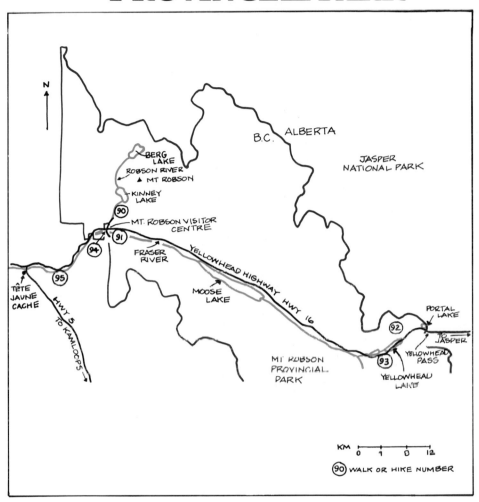

Mt. Robson Provincial Park, the first provincial park established in British Columbia, lies on the western slope of the Canadian Rockies. The park's chief attraction is Mt. Robson, "The Monarch of the Rockies." The 3954 m (12,972 ft) summit rises nearly two vertical miles above the Robson visitor centre.

Walks and easy hikes in the park feature: human history, the Fraser River, and the lush vegetation that results from the higher precipitation on the western slopes of the Rockies.

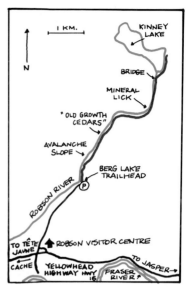

90. **Kinney Lake**

Photo above: Kinney Lake, known as the "mirror of the mount," lies at the foot of Mt. Robson, highest peak in the Canadian Rockies. The lake was named for Reverend George Kinney, who took part in the first attempts to climb the mountain in 1908 and 1909.

Trailhead: Follow Highway 16 to Mt. Robson, 84 km west of Jasper (18 km east of Tete Jaune Cache). Turn north, and follow the road past the Robson visitor centre for 2 km to the parking lot at the Berg Lake trailhead.

Rating: harder, 5.2 km. Brochure available at the visitor centre

Lighting: anytime

The hike to Kinney Lake is along the first 5 km of the Berg Lake Trail. It crosses the Robson River and follows its west bank, climbing gradually to the outlet of the lake. The wide trail is well suited to families. Please use caution; it is also popular with mountain bikers.

The vegetation on the hike to Kinney Lake is not typical of the Rockies; it is more typical of a coastal rainforest. The Robson Valley receives one and a half times more precipitation than Jasper townsite. Most of the precipitation results when air is forced to rise over Mt. Robson's 3954 m (12,972 ft) summit. The precipitation and the longer growing season at this low elevation (860 m, 2828 ft) create a lush forest. The rain forest indicators are the western red cedar, western hemlock, green alder, devil's club, and thimbleberry.

After about a kilometre, the trail crosses an avalanche slope. Here, in late June, you will find one of the best wildflower displays on any trail in this book. Look for western (red) columbine, Indian paintbrush, harebell, spotted saxifrage, false solomon's seal, wild rose, wild strawberry, white geranium, calypso orchid, and cow parsnip.

The rainforest atmosphere of the Kinney Lake hike culminates a kilometre farther, as the trail enters an "old-growth" grove of western red cedar trees. These widely spaced giants are probably 200 to 300 years old. Devil's club, horsetail, queen's cup, and ferns are common on the forest floor.

After leaving the cedar grove, the trail bends to the right, revealing a view of Mt. Resplendent, second highest mountain in the park. It then crosses another avalanche slope created in 1968. Although the park brochure characterizes avalanches as "the worst scourges of mountain regions," they are natural processes that help create new growth by opening sections of forest.

Three kilometres from the trailhead, a boardwalk keeps the hiker's feet out of a mineral lick – damp soils that contain a high concentration of salts and minerals. Look for the tracks of elk, deer, moose, and mountain goats. They come to this lick for a nutritional boost. The tall shrub, red elderberry, grows nearby.

The outlet of Kinney Lake is a kilometre farther. To reach the viewpoint overlooking the lake, cross the bridge and continue up the switchbacks to the top of a bluff. A boardwalk leads left to the viewpoint. Across the blue-green waters are the avalanche scarred slopes of Cinnamon Peak. To the north is Whitehorn Mountain.

Western Red Cedar

The western red cedar, the provincial tree emblem of British Columbia, usually grows to be the tallest of the 17 tree species in the Rockies. Its straight 40 m trunk has shreddy gray bark in vertical strips. The leaves of this evergreen conifer are frond-like, scaly, and flat.

The cedar's soft, fragrant wood is resistant to rot, which has made it a popular choice with builders. Natives of the west coast used it for totem poles, dugout canoes, boxes, and clothing. Contemporary carpenters desire cedar for shingles, fence posts, siding, and boat timbers. Unfortunately, this tree has been subject to overcutting. Soon the only old-growth pockets may be those that exist in protected areas such as Mt. Robson Provincial Park.

91. **Overlander Falls**

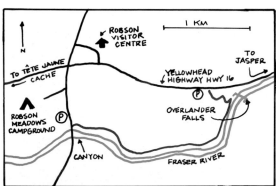

Trailheads: Highway 16, 19.6 km east of Tete Jaune Cache and 1.6 km east of the Robson visitor centre; 80.4 km west of Jasper. Or Fraser River bridge, 500 m south of Robson Meadows Campground.

Ratings: From Highway 16: easy, 500 m. From Fraser River bridge: moderate, 1.9 km

Lighting: afternoon

Overlander Falls commemorates the epic journey of a group of gold seekers, who crossed Canada in 1862. This 10 m high waterfall on the Fraser River can be reached by two trails. For those with sufficient time, take the trail that begins on the north side of the bridge, south of Robson Meadows Campground. The trail winds along the steep banks of the river, and you can visit the ruins of a camp used during construction of the Grand Trunk Pacific Railway. If you desire a shorter outing, take the pleasant downhill walk from Highway 16.

The Fraser River is one of the longest in western North America. From its source on the Continental Divide, southeast of Yellowhead Pass, it flows 1280 km to the Pacific Ocean at Vancouver. The Fraser River drains 145,000 sq km of British Columbia. It is named for Simon Fraser, an explorer and trader with the North West Company, who followed the river from Prince George to the ocean in 1808. The river is noted for its tumultuous rapids.

In 1858, word reached the outside world of gold discovered along the Fraser, and in the Cariboo Mountains, west of the Rockies. Various agencies in eastern Canada enticed would-be gold miners from Europe with their transportation arrangements and promised to deliver them to the motherlode.

In 1862, a group of 125 from Liverpool departed from Toronto for the gold country. Their travel arrangements broke down at Fort Garry (now Winnipeg), and the travellers were left to fend for themselves. Together with some locals, The Overlanders, as they became known, set out for Edmonton in a wagon train. From there, they tackled the crossing of the Rockies on foot, via the Athabasca, Miette, and Fraser valleys. Frequently short of supplies, they resorted to butchering their cattle and horses, and shooting skunk, porcupine, and chipmunks to provide rations.

The Overlanders split into two groups. The ardent gold seekers

rafted the Fraser River to Quesnel (kwuh-NELL). At least six of them drowned. Those who had (understandably) lost the gold fever walked south to Kamloops. After the tribulations of their 5600 km five-month journey, most of The Overlanders could not face the further privations of the Cariboo goldfields, so they continued to the Pacific coast.

Overlander Falls is an insurmountable barrier to migrating chinook salmon from the Pacific. Were it not for the falls, the salmon might be able to reach the headwaters of the Fraser River.

Photo opposite: Overlander Falls cascade over a 10 metre ledge on the Fraser River. The falls are named for a group of gold seekers, The Overlanders, who crossed western Canada by wagon, by raft, and on foot in 1862.

Dwarf Dogwood

Dwarf dogwood is one of the most common and attractive wildflowers in both the Rockies and Canada. It grows in damp, mossy areas of shaded forests. The prominent white "petals" are not part of the flower, but are modified leaves called bracts. The minuscule flowers are pale green and yield a brilliant cluster of red berries in late summer — hence the other common name, bunchberry. Look for dwarf dogwood in the vicinity of Overlander Falls, along with three other common flowers of the coniferous forest: wild strawberry, queen's cup, and twinflower.

OTHER WALKS AND HIKES IN MT. ROBSON PROVINCIAL PARK

See map on page 143

92. Portal Lake

Trailhead: Picnic area at Yellowhead Pass on Highway 16 (23 km west of Jasper; 61 km east of Robson visitor centre; 79 km east of Tete Jaune Cache).
Rating: easy, 500 m
Lighting: anytime

A short stroll at Portal Lake is an ideal way to stretch your legs and rest after driving on the Yellowhead Highway. The trail follows the east shore of the lake, and climbs onto a rocky knoll covered in a doghair forest of lodgepole pine. Although it is possible to loop back to the highway along the provincial boundary cutline, it is a poorly defined and frustrating route. It is best to retrace your route back to the parking lot along the lakeshore. Yellow pond lilies grow in the lake.

93. Labrador Tea Trail

Trailhead: Opposite Site 2 in the Lucerne Campground. Highway 16 (34 km west of Jasper; 50 km east of Robson visitor centre; 68 km east of Tete Jaune Cache).
Rating: easy, 2.5 km loop
Lighting: anytime

The Labrador Tea Trail (also called Yellowhead Lake Trail) loops through a shaded pine forest to the shore of Yellowhead Lake. Interpretive signs describe vegetation on the forest floor. Labrador tea is an evergreen shrub with showy white flowers. Its leaves were used by Natives and explorers to make a strong tea.

94. Fraser River Nature Trail

Trailhead: Site 39 in the Robson Meadows Campground. Follow Highway 16 (84 km west of Jasper; 18 km east of Tete Jaune Cache). Enter the campground, which is 1 km south of the Robson visitor centre.
Rating: easy, 2 km loop
Lighting: anytime

This pleasant nature walk to the banks of the Fraser is an ideal outing for those staying in the campground. Interpretive signs describe the common vegetation.

95. Rearguard Falls

Trailhead: Follow Highway 16 (90 km west of Jasper; 6 km west of Robson visitor centre; 12 km east of Tete Jaune Cache).
Rating: easy, 300 m
Lighting: afternoon

Rearguard Falls is a spectacular river-wide rapid on the Fraser. These falls are the last barrier that can be surmounted by chinook salmon returning from the Pacific to spawn. Look for them here in August and September.

Walks for the Elderly and Young Families

The following walks are recommended to the elderly and to families with young children. Walk numbers are indicated in parentheses.

Akamina Lake (**89**)
Annette Lake (**35**)
Athabasca Falls (**43**)
Bankhead (**6**)
Beaver Lake (**52**)
Bison Paddock Viewpoint (**83**)
Bow Falls (**1**)
Bow Lake (**19**)
Bow River (**29**)
Bow Summit (**20**)
Cameron Falls and
    Waterton Townsite (**78**)
Cameron Lake (**81**)
Centennial Trail (**64**)
Deerlodge (**69**)
Discovery Trail (**26**)
Emerald Lake (**57**)
Fenland Trail (**4**)
Fireweed Trail (**70**)
Fraser River Nature Trail (**94**)
Hamilton Falls (**67**)
Johnson Lake (**23**)
Johnston Canyon
    – lower falls (**11**)
Kootenai Brown's Grave (**84**)
Labrador Tea (**93**)
Lac Beauvert (**50**)
Lake Louise Shoreline (**13**)
Linnet Lake (**85**)
Maligne Canyon – loop: teahouse to
    second bridge (**36**)
Maligne Lake – use lakeshore trail
    for return (**37**)
Marble Canyon (**72**)
Marsh Trail (**3**)
Miette Boardwalk (**64**)

Mistaya Canyon (**21**)
Montane Trail (**10**)
Moraine Lake Lakeshore (**30**)
Moraine Lake Rockpile (**16**)
Natural Bridge (**66**)
Ochre Beds and Paint Pots (**73**)
Overlander Falls
    – from Hwy. 16 (**91**)
Path of the Glacier (**40**)
Pocahontas – lower trail (**38**)
Portal Lake (**92**)
Prince of Wales (**86**)
Rearguard Falls (**95**)
Red Rock Canyon and
    Blakiston Falls (**82**)
Spiral Tunnel Viewpoint (**63**)
Stewart Canyon (**7**)
Sunwapta Falls (**47**)
Takakkaw Falls (**55**)
The Great Divide (**60**)
Tunnel Mountain Hoodoos (**5**)
Valleyview (**76**)
Wapta Falls (**59**)

Metric/Imperial Conversion Table

1 centimetre (cm)	0.394 inches
1 metre (m)	3.28 feet
1 kilometre (km)	0.62 miles
1 hectare (ha)	2.47 acres
1 square kilometre (sq km)	0.386 square miles
1 kilogram (kg)	2.205 pounds
1 tonne	0.9842 UK tons
	1.102 US tons
1 litre (l)	0.22 Imp. gallons
	0.264 US gallons
1° Celsius (C)	1.8° Fahrenheit

0° Celsius = 32° Fahrenheit

Wheelchair Accessible Trails

The following trails are wheelchair accessible, although in some instances, natural and man-made barriers preclude access to the full trail length. Inclines are usually present, and an assistant is recommended. Walk numbers are indicated in parentheses.

Annette Lake (**35**)
Athabasca Falls (**43**)
Beaver Lake (**52**)
Bison Paddock Viewpoint (**83**)
Bow Falls (**1**)
Bow Lake (**19**)
Bow River (**29**)
Bow Summit – from the
    upper parking lot (**20**)
Cameron Falls and Waterton
    Townsite (**78**)
Deerlodge (**69**)
Emerald Lake – west shore,
    first 2 km (**57**)
Fenland Trail (**4**)
Great Divide (**60**)
Johnston Canyon
    – lower falls (**11**)
Kootenai Brown's Grave (**84**)
Lac Beauvert – west shore (**50**)
Lake Louise Shoreline (**13**)
Linnet Lake (**85**)
Maligne Canyon – loop: tea-house
    to second bridge (**36**)
Maligne Lake (**37**)
Marsh Trail (**3**)
Miette Boardwalk (**54**)
Natural Bridge (**66**)
Pocahontas (**38**)
Red Rock Canyon (**82**)
Spiral Tunnel Viewpoint (**63**)
Sundance Canyon
    – first 3.8 km (**27**)
Sunwapta Falls – use path at east
    edge of parking lot (**47**)
Takakkaw Falls (**55**)
The Great Divide (**60**)
The Whistlers – tramway to
    boardwalk at upper terminal (**39**)
Tunnel Mountain Hoodoos (**5**)

Walks and Easy Hikes from Campgrounds

Many of these trails are ideal for after-dinner outings or as rainy-day diversions. Walk numbers are in parentheses.

Campground	Walk
Bow Valley	Montane Trail (**10**)
Castle Mountain	Silverton Falls (**28**)
Columbia Icefield	Wilcox Pass (**45**)
Crandell	Crandell Lake (**88**)
Hoodoo Creek	Deerlodge (**69**)
	Leanchoil Hoodoos (**58**)
Johnston Canyon	Johnston Canyon (**11**)
Kicking Horse	A Walk in the Past (**56**)
	Centennial Trail (**64**)
Lucerne	Labrador Tea
	(Yellowhead Lake) (**93**)
McLeod Meadows	Dog Lake (**75**)
Pocahontas	Pocahontas/
	Punchbowl Falls (**38**)
Redstreak	Redstreak (Aquacourt) (**77**)
	Valleyview (**76**)
Robson Meadows	Fraser River (**94**)
	Overlander Falls (**91**)
Takakkaw Falls	Laughing Falls (**65**)
	Takakkaw Falls (**55**)
Tunnel Mountain	Tunnel Mountain
	Hoodoos (**5**)
Waterton Townsite	Cameron Falls (**78**)
	Linnet Lake (**85**)
	Lower Bertha Falls (**79**)
	Prince of Wales (**86**)
Wilcox Creek	Wilcox Pass (**45**)

Useful Telephone Numbers

In an emergency, dial "0" and ask the operator for the Royal Canadian Mounted Police, fire department, or ambulance. The area code in Alberta is 403. In British Columbia it is 604.

Banff and the Bow Valley
Banff Information Centre
    403-762-4256
Banff Warden Office
    403-762-4506
Bow Valley Provincial Park
    403-673-3663

Jasper National Park
Jasper Townsite Information Centre
    403-852-6176
Jasper Warden Office
    403-852-0150
Sunwapta Warden Office
    (Icefields Parkway, Jasper)
    403-852-6181

Kootenay National Park
Kootenay Information Centre
    604-347-9505
Kootenay Warden Office
    604-347-9361

Lake Louise to Columbia Icefield
Columbia Icefield Information
    Centre 403-852-2241
Lake Louise Information Centre
    403-522-3833
Lake Louise Warden Office
    403-522-3866

Mt. Robson Provincial Park
Mt. Robson Provincial Park:
    604-546-4325

Waterton Lakes National Park
Waterton Park Information Centre
    403-859-2445
Waterton Warden Office
    403-859-2477

Yoho National Park
Yoho Information Centre
    604-343-6324
Yoho Warden Office
    604-343-6324

Weather
Banff
    403-762-2088
Jasper
    403-852-3185

The Author's Favourite Walks and Easy Hikes

Athabasca Falls (**43**)	Maligne Canyon (**36**)
Athabasca Glacier (**44**)	Marble Canyon (**72**)
Bear's Hump (**80**)	Moraine Lake
Bison Paddock	Rockpile (**16**)
Viewpoint (**83**)	Ochre Beds and
Bow Summit (**20**)	Paint Pots (**73**)
Cavell Meadows (**41**)	Parker Ridge (**22**)
Emerald Lake (**57**)	Path of the Glacier (**40**)
Fenland Trail (**4**)	Stanley Glacier (**71**)
Johnston Canyon (**11**)	Takakkaw Falls (**55**)
Lake Louise	The Whistlers (**39**)
Shoreline (**13**)	Wilcox Pass (**45**)

Recommended Field Guides

General

Gadd, Ben. *Handbook of the Canadian Rockies*. Jasper: Corax Press, 1986. The most comprehensive field guide available

Kavanagh, James. *Nature Alberta*. Edmonton: Lone Pine Publishing, 1991. Birds, animals, trees, shrubs, and wildflowers of the eastern slopes of the Rockies

Pole, Graeme. *Canadian Rockies SuperGuide*. Banff: Altitude Publishing, 1991. A motorist's guide to the Rocky Mountain parks

Bird-watching

Van Tighem, Kevin and Andrew LeMessurier. *Birding Jasper National Park*. Jasper: Parks and People, 1989

Scotter, G.W., T. J. Ulrich, and E.T. Jones. *Birds of the Canadian Rockies*. Saskatoon: Western Producer Prairie Books, 1990. Excellent photography

Peterson, R.T. *A Field Guide to the Western Birds*. Boston: Houghton Mifflin, 3rd edition, 1989. The standard reference for western North America

Holroyd, G.L. and Howard Coneybare. *Birds of the Rockies*. Edmonton: Lone Pine Publishing, 1990. Illustrations

Wildflowers

Scotter, George W. and Hälle Flygare. *Wildflowers of the Canadian Rockies*. Edmonton: Hurtig Publishers, 1986. Colour photography

Porsild, A.E. and Dagny Tande Lid. *Rocky Mountain Wildflowers*. Ottawa: National Museum of Natural Sciences, 1979. Illustrations

Craighead J., F.C. Craighead, Jr., and R.J. Davis. *Rocky Mountain Wildlfowers*. Boston: Houghton Mifflin, 1963. Covers the American Rockies too. Colour photography

Animals

Burt, W.H. and R.P. Grossenheider. *Mammals*. Boston: Houghton Mifflin, 3rd edition, 1980. The standard Peterson guide to mammals

Van Tighem, Kevin. *Wild Animals of Western Canada*. Banff: Altitude Publishing, 1992

Schmidt, D. and E. Schmidt. *Alberta Wildlife Viewing Guide*. Edmonton: Lone Pine Publishing, 1990

Ulrich, T.J. *Mammals of the Northern Rockies*. Missoula: Mountain Press, ca. 1988

Tips for 35 mm Photography

• Lighting is the stuff of which good landscape photographs are made. If you have a particular photographic destination in mind, carefully consider the time of day and the resulting angle of light. To help plan your itinerary, use the "lighting" information given for each trail.

• The photographer taking sunrise and sunset photographs should be prepared to make some adjustments while in the mountains. The horizon is blocked in most locations. And the best effects are not obtained by including the sun in the photograph, but by capturing the colourful lighting in the opposite direction. Called alpenglow, this light precedes sunrise and follows sunset. Underexpose slightly, to saturate colours at these times of day.

• Much of the year, snow will be present in most scenes. You will frequently encounter difficult lighting situations, incorporating opposing values of sunlit snow and shado. Bracketing exposures is recommended. Often the best results for slide film will be achieved by under-exposing slightly when photographing a bright and uniformly lit landscape scene that includes snow. (Underexposing is not recommended for print film.)

• To obtain facial details of people in the foreground of bright landscapes, take a close-up light meter reading of the person's face, then use this exposure for the scene. In some cases, the extraordinary contrast between the foreground and background go beyond the limits of the slide film. At these times, expose for the background and try infilling the foreground with flash, or use a graduated filter to darken the brightest part of the scene.

• Kodachrome 64 and 200 films are the most versatile for most applications in Rocky Mountain photography. (All of the colour photographs in this book were recorded on these films.) If you have two camera bodies and can dedicate one to each type of film, you will achieve tremendous flexibility with regard to lighting, depth of field, and colour saturation.

• Although smog, firesmoke, and haze are not common in the Rockies, exposed film will register a higher incidence of ultraviolet light because of the altitude. A UV (ultraviolet) filter will help reduce the resulting bluish cast. Compositions involving water, ice, and clouds may benefit if you experiment with a polarizing filter.

• A selection of lenses spanning the range from 24-300 mm is indispensable to the nature photographer in the Rockies. A tripod is also essential. Carry lots of film. Fingerless gloves or thin glove liners help take the chill out of early morning and late evening shoots.

• Watch for condensation and frost on lens elements when stepping from a warm vehicle into the cold outdoors. On really cold mornings, hold your breath when releasing the shutter, so as not to get vapour in the foreground.

• Keep your equipment lightweight, accessible, and well-organized. You will be more inclined to carry it with you. Insure your camera is ready with the lens best suited to the kind of photograph you seek (for example: telephoto for wildlife; wide angle for landscape). This will minimize set-up time when a good scene presents itself.

• Think ahead to anticipate lighting, and linger a while if things are not initially favourable for photography. As with most endeavors, patience with photography usually pays off.

Glossary

The numbers in parentheses refer to the walks and hikes where these features are found.

Alluvial fan (ah-LOO-vee-ull) A fan-shaped deposit of sediment created where a steep mountain stream enters a slow stream or broad valley. (**9, 19, 57, 80**)

Alpine ecoregion The vegetation zone above treeline, characterized by rocky soils and scattered low-lying wildflowers, lichens, and mosses. (**12, 22, 39, 45**)

Arête A narrow, rugged mountain ridge. In the Rockies arêtes often separate cirques. (**22**)

Avalanche An accumulation of snow that sweeps down a mountainside, sometimes accompanied by rock debris and vegetation. (**15, 22, 57, 64, 81**)

Bedrock Solid rock outcrops on the surface, or the solid rock underlying loose surface materials (boulders, gravel, and sand), soils, and vegetation.

Chinook (shih-NOOK) In the Rockies, a warm wind that blows eastward from the mountains toward the prairies. (**5, 10, 78**)

Cirque (SURK) The bowl-shaped depression created by glacial erosion on a mountainside. The walls of the cirque are created through downward and backward erosion by the moving ice. (**15, 81**)

Cirque glacier A small glacier occupying a cirque. (**15, 22, 40**)

Climax species The species of trees and other vegetation that culminate the process of succession. In the montane forest, this would be Douglas fir and white spruce. (**4, 70**)

Continental Divide In the Canadian Rockies, the mountain ridge that separates water flowing east and north to the Atlantic and Arctic oceans from water flowing west to the Pacific. (**12, 60**)

CPR (Canadian Pacific Railway) Canada's first transcontinental railway, constructed in the Rockies between 1882 and 1884. The railway helped develop the tourist industry that led to the establishment of Banff and Yoho national parks. (**5, 6, 14, 37, 56, 57, 58, 60, 63**)

Delta A fan-shaped deposit of sediment at the mouth of a river, created from sediments that drop out as the current slows down. (**14, 15, 19, 20, 44, 57**)

Doghair forest A dense forest of lodgepole pine of uniform age, created by thick seeding after a forest fire. (**70, 92**)

Dolomite A kind of limestone rock that has a high amount of both lime and magnesium. (**11, 72**)

Douglas fir One of the trees typical of the montane ecoregion. It grows on dry south-facing slopes. Characteristics: coniferous, 30 to 40 m tall, straight or gracefully curving trunk, and furrowed and cork-like bark. (**2, 42, 51, 58, 68, 76**)

Eastern Main Ranges The mountain ranges along the Continental Divide between Banff and Yellowhead Pass. (**35, 36**)

Ecoregion An ecological and vegetation zone. There are three ecoregions in the Rockies: montane, subalpine, and alpine. The boundaries between them are not precise, varying with local climate and topography. (**10, 12, 20, 22, 39, 41**)

Engelmann spruce One of the two most common trees in the subalpine ecoregion. Characteristics: coniferous, 20 to 30 m tall, reddish-brown and shreddy bark, and spikey and squarish needles that roll between your fingers. George Engelmann was a 19th century botanist. (**13, 15, 20, 22, 41, 45, 81**)

Erratic A rock or boulder transported from its place of origin by glacial ice. (**36, 39, 72**)

Fault A fracture in the rock of the earth's surface, where rock on one side of the fracture has moved relative to rock on the other side. (**1, 7, 10, 11, 35, 36, 43**)

Feather mosses Leafless, rootless plants that prefer damp, shaded locations. Common on the floor of the subalpine forest. (**13, 15, 58**)

Fen A lowland area covered partially or entirely by water. (**4**)

Foothills Hills on the east slope of the Rockies. (**10**)

Forefield The area immediately in front of a glacier. Covered by glacial ice less than 150 years ago and characterized by rubble, meltwater streams, and scant vegetation. (**14, 19, 40, 44**)

Formation Distinctive layers of rock, representing a particular kind of past environment. For example, a formation like the Burgess shale is what remains from the deposition of sediments on the floor of an ancient sea millions of years ago.

Formations are often named after areas where they are prominent or where they were first studied. (**10, 14, 16, 36, 38, 42, 43, 59, 72, 78**)

Front Ranges The easternmost mountain ranges of the Rockies. (**10, 35, 36, 80, 83**)

Frost hollow A shallow depression where cold air collects, stunting the growth of vegetation. Common next to glaciers and at the mouths of mountainside streams. (**17, 18, 22**)

Glacial landforms Landforms created by glaciers and glacial streams. Glacial landforms that are made of sediment include: moraines (**10, 14, 40, 44, 81**), drumlins (**10, 83**), eskers (**10, 83, 87**), kames (**10, 83, 86**), and kettle ponds (**10, 35, 48, 83**).

Glacier A mass of ice formed from consolidated snow and moving slowly downhill under its own weight. (**14, 40, 44**)

Hanging valley In the Rockies, a tributary valley that glacial ice did not erode as deeply as the adjacent major valley. Hence the mouth of the hanging valley "hangs" above the major valley. (**21, 27, 36, 55**)

Hoodoo A natural column of rock or sediment. In the Bow and Yoho valleys hoodoos are resistant pillars of glacial till. (**5, 9, 58**)

Hot spring A natural outlet for groundwater that has been heated deep beneath the earth's surface. (**3, 54, 73**)

Icefield An expansive flat area of glacial ice. In the Canadian Rockies they are found at elevations above 2420 m (8000 ft). (**19, 20, 44, 55**)

Interior plains The extensive flat area of central North America.

Karst Underground drainage in limestone bedrock created by chemical action and flowing water. In the Rockies, karst is characterized by hidden streams, canyons, caves, and sinkholes. (**36, 45**)

Kettle pond A lake that fills a hollow created by a slump in the underlying glacial rubble, usually from the melting of a block of ice. (**10, 35, 48, 83**)

Krummholz Gnarled and stunted forms of Engelmann spruce, subalpine fir, whitebark pine, lodgepole pine, and Lyall's larch. Found at treeline, on cliff edges, or near glaciers. (**12, 20, 22**)

Lateral moraine A ridge of glacial till pushed up alongside a glacier. (**14, 40, 44**)

Limestone Sedimentary rock created from deposits of lime or from the skeletal remains of marine life. (**8, 9, 11, 16, 36**)

Little Ice Age A minor, global glacial advance that lasted from 1200 A.D. until the late 1800s. (**14, 40, 44**)

Lodgepole pine One of the common trees of the montane ecoregion. Characteristics: coniferous, 5 to 20 m tall, straight trunk (often with no lower branches), needles in pairs, and scaly grey bark (often with a reddish-orange hue). Cones are sealed with resin and must be cracked open by fire for effective seeding. (**70**)

Lyall's larch (LIE-ulls) A tree of the upper subalpine ecoregion. Characteristics: coniferous, 5 to 10 m tall, ragged looking, and with pale green needles (needles turn golden and are shed in autumn). (**17, 18**)

Marginal lake A lake that forms immediately in front of a glacier. (**22, 44, 55**)

Montane ecoregion The vegetation zone in the major valley bottoms and on lower mountainsides. Typical vegetation includes Douglas fir, white spruce, and lodgepole pine. (**10, 21, 42**)

Moraine (more-RAIN) A deposit of glacial till. (**10, 14, 19, 20, 40, 44, 47, 57, 59**)

Niche glacier (NEESH) Glacial ice that forms on a minor indentation in a mountainside. Sustained by wind-blown snow. Often peculiar in shape. (**14, 22, 57**)

Outcrop A protrusion of bedrock.

Outlet valley glacier A glacier that flows from an icefield into an adjacent valley. (**14, 22, 44**)

Outwash plain A level area where sediments transported by glacial meltwater accumulate.

Old-growth forest A forest in which the climax species have seeded more than one generation. (**45, 57, 68, 90**)

Overthrust mountain In the front ranges of the Rockies, a mountain with a steeply tilted southwest-facing slope, whose top ends on a northeast-facing cliff. (**2**)

Palliser Expedition An expedition sent by the British government in 1857, to explore central and western Canada. (**9, 18, 43, 59, 82**)

Plunge pool A rounded depression in the bedrock beneath a waterfall, resulting from the incessant pounding of water. (**11, 38, 72**)

Potholes Circular depressions drilled into the bedrock near falls and rapids by boulders trapped in eddies and backwaters. (11, 21, 36, 43, 72, 82)

Quartzite A kind of altered quartz-rich sandstone. The quartz particles have liquefied and then reconsolidated, binding the rock together. (16, 14, 35, 43)

Rock flour Rock particles (silt) produced by glacial erosion that are so tiny that they are suspended in glacial lake water. These particles reflect the blue and green wavelengths of light, giving the lakes their colour. (20)

Rock lichens Rootless, leafless plants that grow on rocks and cliffs. (17, 22)

Sandstone A rock made from sand grains. Often, many of these are quartz. (16, 42)

Sediment Solids including rock, mineral, soil, or chemical material transported from elsewhere and deposited by wind, water, or glaciers. (16, 78)

Sedimentary rock Rock formed from the accumulation of sediments. The sediments can originate from the erosion of other rocks (sandstone, shale, conglomerate, gritstone, siltstone, and tillite) from chemical action (limestone and dolomite), or from the accumulation of skeletal remains such as in coral reefs (limestone). (16, 36, 38, 42)

Strike valley A valley formed along a linear geographical feature. In the Rockies, one kind of valley formed by erosion into the interface between two thrust sheets. (7, 36)

Subalpine ecoregion The vegetation zone between the montane and alpine ecoregions and home of the subalpine forest. Found on mountainsides and in valley bottoms at higher elevations. (13, 15, 20, 22, 41, 81)

Subalpine fir One of two common trees in the subalpine ecoregion. Characteristics: coniferous, 20 to 30 m tall, conical shape with a spire-like crown, silvery bark with resin blisters, and branches curling upwards. (13, 15, 20, 22, 41, 81)

Subalpine forest The forest occupying the subalpine ecoregion on mountainsides and high valleys in the Rockies (1400–2300 m elevation). Typical vegetation: subalpine fir, Lyall's larch, whitebark pine, and feather mosses. (13, 15, 20, 81)

Succession A natural process of change from youth to maturity in a vegetation community. (1, 4, 39, 70)

Syncline A U-shaped fold in layered rock, produced by compressive forces during mountain building. (43)

Tarn A small mountain lake or pond. In the Rockies, tarns are often in hollows scoured from the bedrock by glacial ice. Tarns are frequently fed by glacial meltwater and dammed by moraines. (15, 17, 19)

Terminal moraine A horseshoe-shaped ridge of till pushed up by a glacier and marking the maximum extent of a glacial advance. (19, 40, 44, 57, 81)

Terminus The lower end, or toe, of a glacier. (44)

Thrust fault A surface along which an assemblage of rock has slid upwards and over adjacent rock. The fault was created by compressive forces during mountain building. (**2, 10, 11, 78**)

Thrust sheet The assemblage of rock that slides along a thrust fault. (**10, 78, 80**)

Till Rock fragments of many sizes (from rock flour to giant boulders) deposited by glaciers. (**5, 44, 58**)

Tillite Till that has become rock. In the Bow valley till has been cemented by lime forming a natural concrete. (**5, 58**)

Tree lichens Rootless, leafless plants that grow on tree trunks and branches. (**58**)

Treeline The upper limit of tree growth, separating the subalpine from the alpine ecoregion. In the Canadian Rockies at an elevation of about 2200 m (7220 ft) on south-facing slopes; lower on north-facing slopes or near glaciers. (**18, 20, 22, 39, 41**)

Tufa In the Rockies, usually a crumbly limestone rock, created by chemical action at the outlet of a mineral spring. (**3, 26**)

Tundra A treeless area at high elevation or near glaciers. Vegetation includes wildflowers, low-growing shrubs, sedges, mosses, and rock lichens. (**12, 22, 41, 45**)

U-shaped valley A valley that has been eroded or enlarged by glacial ice. Also called a trough. (**5, 43, 55, 71, 80**)

Vascular plant Plants that circulate sap and fluid through a vessel system: trees, shrubs, grasses, sedges, and flowers. (**12**)

Western red cedar A rare tree in the Rockies, found only in areas of very wet climate. Characteristics: coniferous, up to 40 m tall, scaly and frond-like leaves, grey bark that shreds in vertical strips, and aromatic wood. (**56, 57, 68, 90**)

White spruce A characteristic tree of the montane ecoregion, especially along riverbanks and on flood plains. Similar to Engelmann spruce, with which it hybridizes. (**1, 4**)

Whitebark pine Found on cliff edges and windy locations, usually in the subalpine ecoregion. Characteristics: coniferous, greyish-brown bark, needles in bunches of 5, and branches that flag the prevailing wind. Sometimes grows in krummholz form. (**5, 22**)

Wisconsin Glaciation An ice age that lasted from 75,000 to 11,000 years ago. Ice sheets were over a kilometre thick. There were three distinct advances of glacial ice during this period. Two of these extended from the Rockies eastward to the plains. (**1, 5, 10, 11, 14, 21, 22, 36, 39, 44, 80, 88**)

Index

The names of the walks and easy hikes are indicated in bold.

The Author and Photographer

Graeme Pole lives in Field, B.C. He is a licensed interpretive guide, a seasoned hiker, and a mountaineer. He brings to this work nine years of experience, observation, and research in the Canadian Rockies. Graeme is the author of the *Canadian Rockies SuperGuide*, and the *Canadian Rockies: A History in Photographs*. When not hiking, taking photographs, and writing, Graeme serves with the British Columbia Ambulance Service as an Emergency Medical Assistant and Unit Chief in Field.